# *You Can*
# Write
# A Novel

## JAMES V. SMITH, JR.

**WRITER'S DIGEST BOOKS**
CINCINNATI, OHIO

Other fine Writer's Digest Books are available from your local bookstore or direct from the publisher.

For information on more resources for writers, visit our Web site at www.writers digest.com.

To recieve a free biweekly E-mail newsletter delivering tips and updates about writing and about Writer's Digest products, send an E-mail with "Subscribe Newsletter" in the body of the message to newsletter-request@writersdigest.com, or register directly at our Web site at www.writersdigest.com.

02   01       5   4   3   2

Library of Congress Cataloging-in-Publication Data

Smith, James V.
  You can write a novel / James V. Smith, Jr. —1st ed.
     p.     cm.
  Includes index.
  ISBN 0-89879-868-X (pbk. : alk. paper)
  1. Fiction—Authorship. I. Title.
PN3365.S64 1998
808.3—dc21                                                          98-35880
                                                                          CIP

Edited by David Borcherding
Production edited by Amy J. Wolgemuth
Designed by Mary Barnes Clark

## ABOUT THE AUTHOR

James V. Smith, Jr., has published five novels and three nonfiction books. His latest novels include a three-book military action-adventure series, Force Recon, for Putnam Berkley, the first of which is scheduled for publication in 1999. He is also marketing a mainstream novel about a teacher's personal and professional struggle in dealing with a hostile group of juvenile delinquents inside the walls of a maximum security lockup.

Smith is a former news and feature writer for *The Dallas Morning News* and *The Indianapolis News*. He has published nonfiction articles in *Writer's Digest, The American Legion Magazine,* and *Family Circle*. He is a Gannett Journalism Teaching Fellow of Indiana University. Smith lives in Montana with his wife, Sue, daughter, Katy, and golden retriever, Gus.

**TABLE OF CONTENTS**

# 1 FIND AND REFINE A SALABLE IDEA FOR YOUR NOVEL

## 5 things to think about when you're thinking about ideas for your novel

> Between the idea
> And the reality
> Between the motion
> And the act
> Falls the Shadow.
>
> T.S. Eliot

## STEP 1: IDENTIFY A SALABLE IDEA

All published novels begin with a salable idea. In *Jaws* the idea is this: A great white shark terrorizes a resort until three men hunt down the animal and kill it after a titanic struggle that costs one of the trio his life.

Is your idea as commercial as *Jaws*? Or will it flop? Who knows?

The sad fact of publishing is this: *Nobody* knows. The only certain way to test an idea is to write a finished novel and offer it for sale. The great master himself, Stephen King, submitted three complete novels—all rejected—until he sold his "first novel," *Carrie*.

This book will teach you a step-by-step system for writing and submitting your novel to the publishing industry. Soon enough after you mail the manuscript, agents and editors will tell you what they think. If you get past that hurdle, book buyers will vote with their money. Then you'll know.

For now, forget all about agents, editors and book buyers. Before you even consider them, you must test the salability of your idea on one very important person, the would-be author.

Can you sell your idea to *yourself*?

### The first test of salability

- **Do you feel such passion for the idea** that you feel it *must* be written into a novel?
- **Do you believe you are the only person** capable of telling the story the way it ought to be told?
- **Can you sustain your excitement** over the weeks or even months it may require to mold your idea into a finished novel?
- **Are you knowledgeable enough** to make your story sound authentic? If not, are you willing to research it?

If you can answer yes to all these questions about your idea, you've taken a huge first step toward making your novel salable. If an author doesn't believe in the idea, there's little likelihood a book will ever get finished, let alone published.

But wait. What if you don't even have an idea to test?

Let's deal with that. As a would-be novelist, you fall into one of three categories.

**One. You're consumed with fire** over the best idea for the Great American Novel since *Moby Dick* (which is, after all, the original *Jaws*). If such a blockbuster idea already has you in its grip, skip ahead to step two (see page 4) to test that idea against reality.

**Two. You're beset with too many great ideas.** You might be asking yourself something along the lines of, Should I fictionalize the saga of Aunt Bess tracking down and administering vigilante justice to the con artists who bilked her out of her life savings? Or should I explore a humorous variation on aliens invading earth by writing a novel about Californians swarming to Oklahoma in a kind of reverse of *The Grapes of Wrath*?

No problem. Test both ideas against the questions above and settle on the one that truly inspires. Don't divide your focus. You'll have enough to deal with in writing a single idea into a novel.

**Three. You have no ideas** and no clue how to find one. No big deal. Ideas are overrated anyhow. Anybody can have a great idea. Just ask any published novelist. Every one of them has heard a variation of the following statement: "You wrote a book, huh?" (Spoken in the tone of,

"Well I guess anybody can do it then.") "I ought to write a book myself. I got this great idea about [insert a diatribe here]. Hey, what if I supply the idea and you write the book? We'll go halves on the royalties. Deal?"

Sure thing.

You see the problem? Not everybody can deliver a novel based on an idea, no matter how great it is. That's why publishing houses prefer to buy novels instead of ideas. So, rather than wait for the impetus of a perfect idea to get you going, act on your own. Take something ugly and work with it. Many of the finest diamonds in the world came out of the earth as shapeless lumps. Their true value came to be realized only after shaping, cutting, grinding and polishing.

Here's a checklist to help you find your own rough gem of an idea that can be worked into shape later in this chapter.

## 8 PLACES TO MINE (OR NOT TO MINE) IDEAS
### 1. Don't steal from existing stories
Putting a new spin on existing ideas is risky for two reasons: One, chances are that somebody else is already doing such a story; two, cycles of popularity end without warning. You're better off to start with something fresh.

Above all, don't steal from television—most of the jaded ideas there have been prestolen, many more than once.

### 2. Don't borrow from current events
Fictionalizing actual events from the national news is probably not salable unless you're Dominick Dunne. If it's in the news, some novelist with a track record is already phoning her agent.

### 3. Borrow from yesterday's events
Research the newsmagazines from yesteryear. Many papers feature a "10, 20, 50 and 100 years ago" department. If you hit upon an idea that sounds inviting, research it. If it hasn't been novelized, use it.

### 4. Borrow from Smalltown, America
Find a university library where you can examine small-town newspaper stories that didn't make the national news. Literally thousands of novel ideas are lying unexploited in these places.

### 5. Surf the Internet
No excuses. If you don't have a computer or access to on-line services, you probably know someone who does. Try the local library or school.

Go anywhere on-line, following links, making bookmarks and writing notes to yourself. The explosion of ideas on the Net is a rich resource for thousands of great ideas (and millions of bad ones). With the search engines now available, all you have to do is pick a general topic and continue refining it until you hit on something that warms your blood. You could discover more ideas in an afternoon on the Internet than you could write into novels in a lifetime.

### 6. Write a working title for your novel
Jump ahead to "Choose a Working Title" in chapter two. Let the idea for a novel spring from the title. Then come back to this chapter to test your idea.

### 7. Write the first line of your novel
Write a great first line, then try to grow an entire novel from that seed.

### 8. Fictionalize your own experiences
You may be the best source for your first novel idea. You have a life full of experiences, interests, hobbies, careers and unique qualities. (Don't you?) Which among them could be dramatized and turned into a novel?

## STEP 2: TEST YOUR IDEA AGAINST REALITY: A QUIZ
Put your darling idea to a test of fire. You must be ruthless, for if you don't hold an idea to strict standards at this early stage of your novel, it might falter, withering after you've put in weeks of labor. So be tough on that idea now and spare yourself later grief.

Speaking of realities, you ought to understand a few realities of the publishing industry before you start pecking on a keyboard. Here are the two salient realities about publishing.

**It ain't art—it's bidness.** No one in the business cares about you or your Great American Novel unless he thinks one or both of you can make money for him.

**Next to money, time is the most important commodity in publishing.** As you put together your novel, it's also a good idea to begin formulating a plan for marketing it without wasting an editor's or agent's time.

In fact, it wouldn't be a bad idea to skip ahead and read chapter six, which deals with these two concepts in greater detail. Then come back and take the following quiz and finish writing your novel with the commercial aspects of the art topmost in your mind.

## THE ESSENTIAL ELEMENTS OF A SALABLE NOVEL

Rate your idea on a scale from 1 to 10 on each of the following.

### 1. Does your novel idea feature a truly heroic character?

Is your heroic character (often called the protagonist) energetic, morally upright, fair and likable? Does she always strive to do the right thing, even if her judgment is sometimes flawed? Is she kind to her friends, dogs and old ladies, and stalwart against injustice? Is she unique, transcending every stereotype you've seen on TV and in the movies? Is she striking in a way *other* than physical attributes?

> Mediocre is 1 ──────► 10 is Breathtakingly Heroic

> Your heroic character rates a _____.

### 2. Does your heroic character have a worthy goal?

Heroic characters must be *for* something substantially good and *against* all things evil, yet they ought to struggle with both. How strongly does such a goal matter to the character and to the reader?

> Trivial is 1 ──────► 10 is Heroically Worthy

> Your heroic character's goal rates a _____.

### 3. Does your heroic character have a worthy adversary?

Adversary, villain, nemesis, antagonist, antihero, obstacle—you get the idea. Whether the heroic character is fighting velociraptors, mobsters, natural disasters, alien visitors or fatal personal errors, is she constantly thrown up against impossible odds? What's the toughness of the competition?

> Cream Puff is 1 ──────► 10 is Heroically Worthy

> Your heroic character's adversary rates a _____.

### 4. Does your idea embody plentiful action and conflict?

We're not simply talking car chases and explosions. Rather, do you envision a novel packed with descriptions of static situations, or does it come alive with clashes personal, internal, external and eternal? Do characters interact rather than muse incessantly? Does the story move toward a conclusion? What's the pace of your novel?

Catatonic is 1 ⟶ 10 is Heroically Animated

Your novel's activity level rates a _____.

### 5. Do you already have a heroic ending in mind?

The ending includes a final, epic struggle between your heroic character and her worthy adversary. Have you planned a powerful physical, emotional or mental dilemma that will be resolved in the heroic character's favor? Does she learn a lesson that is worthwhile and meaningful to the rest of us mortals? How's your ending?

So What? is 1 ⟶ 10 is Heroic

Your novel's ending rates a _____.

## *Scoring your idea*

Let's compare your idea's score to a few criteria that add to or diminish your total.

**The heroic character.** If you didn't start with an 8 or 9, you don't yet have a character worth reading about. Stop right here and go back to square one. Either come up with a fresh idea or revise your heroic character. Same deal if you scored this element a 10. Perfect characters aren't as believable as ones with flaws and an Achilles' heel—even Superman has his kryptonite. Add a fatal flaw to your main character so the reader can more easily identify with her. Give her a weakness so crucial that if she succumbs to it, she's in danger of destroying herself. She might be a recovering alcoholic, for example. Once your character is flawed, add 5 points, bringing your total to 13 or 14.

However, if, as in *Lonesome Dove*, you have multiple heroic characters who share the load of carrying the story, subtract 2 points for a second main character, 3 for a third and so on. If you have as many main characters as in the film *The Big Chill*, you'll end up with a score below zero.

If your heroic character has a love interest, add 3 points. Romance sells novels, even in so-called "boy books."

If your heroine has a unique career or distinctive view of life, add a point for each. If she has a wry sense of humor, add 5 points. If that sense of humor is too smart-alecky, subtract 3.

If your hero dies at the end of the book, subtract 59 points for using such poor judgment as a first novelist. Don't cite the character Gus, in

*Lonesome Dove*, unless you're Larry McMurtry himself. Just return to "Go" and start all over again.

When you've finished calculating, your score should be no less than 16, no more than 24. Anywhere in that range gives you a heroic character that you can work with.

**Your character's goal.** If it isn't in the range of 8 to 10, elevate it somehow. The heroine must strive for more than the perfect parking place, as does George Costanza on *Seinfeld*. Readers ought to care about what a heroic character is battling for or against. If you rated the goal a 10, which is out of reach of most people, give yourself a bonus of 2; but, if the goal you set seems impossible, give yourself a 5 instead. Worry about writing out of that impossible situation later. You can't make things too hard on a heroic character if you want to sell your novel. Your score on this element should now be between 10 and 15. If it's lower, reconsider the toughness of the goal. If it's higher, I admire your imagination, if not your math. Let it stand.

**Your character's adversary.** If the antagonist isn't rated 8 or 9, your heroic character might not be challenged. If you gave your adversary a higher starting score than your main character, add 2 points for envisioning extreme difficulties. But if you gave the antihero a 10, subtract 2. Don't create a villain with no saving grace whatsoever. Even the most vile adversary ought to at least be kind to his mother.

Avoiding the pitfalls I've pointed out, redefine your concept of an adversary until the adjusted score ranges from 10 to 11.

**Your story's action and conflict.** If you don't envision a novel with a pace equal to a range of 8 to 10, you might as well be writing a phone book. Every scene should be filled with tension and action. Keep description to a minimum—in the hands of an amateur, it can induce reader narcolepsy.

UCLA Professor Richard Walter (*Screenwriting*, Plume) wrote screenwriting's lone unbreakable rule: "Don't be boring." My take on that succinct advice:

---

**Cardinal Rule #1:** Never be boring, not for one scene, paragraph, sentence or word.

---

This rule leads into . . .

> **Cardinal Rule #2:** Every writing rule in the book has an exception—except for Cardinal Rule #1.

**Your ending.** Do you even have your ending? If not, go to jail. Stay there until you develop one. Here I borrow from Stephen Covey, author of *The Seven Habits of Highly Effective People*. His first rule for effectiveness, becomes our . . .

> **Cardinal Rule #3:** Begin with the end in mind.

You wouldn't dream of striking out on a journey to Saco, Montana, Mosquito Capital of North America, without pulling out a map and identifying the destination. Why on earth would you begin a first novel without knowing where you'll arrive in the end?

Having the climactic scene in mind at the outset is crucial to writing your novel. Visualizing the climax gives you a target and keeps your novel on track. It becomes the measure by which you decide to keep a scene, a paragraph, a sentence or a word. When you're finished writing, the climactic scene should prove to be the point of the most intense conflict and action, the moment at which all that has come before is aimed, and the point from which the ending is the natural result.

So the climax must be even more powerful than the opening. Add 3 points if you have imagined a climactic scene as the zenith of action and excitement for your novel, even more important than your opening. If your heroic character comes away unscathed, subtract 2, for that's a fairy tale. If she is scarred but wiser for the experience, add 2. If the villain is not vanquished, subtract 3. If the outcome of your novel is decided by a coincidence, act of God or quirky force or character at the last moment, subtract 99 points from your score and start over. Your heroic character alone and no outside cavalry can determine the outcome of a salable novel. In the end, you should have a score of 14 or higher.

## Final scoring

When you've finished this exercise, you must have the minimum score for each element. It doesn't matter what the total numbers are because every individual area must be strong. Nothing much matters for elements two through five, for instance, if your main character is a repulsive slug of a man and a serial rapist besides. Not even John Updike could make a hero out of such a soul. The reality for a first novelist is this:

> **Cardinal Rule #4:** If you don't envision a truly heroic character with heroic goals, on an action-packed journey, encountering obstacles and a worthy opponent and arriving alive and wiser at the end of your novel after having engaged in a titanic struggle, it's not likely your novel will be seriously considered in the publishing business.

Continue noodling your idea until you meet the philosophical standard set in rule number four. Then move on.

## STEP 3: REFINE YOUR IDEA INTO A WRITTEN "NUGGET" STATEMENT

State your idea in no more than 35 to 40 words. This is practically done for you if you've faithfully tested your idea against reality in the previous step. The point of this exercise is to create the first hard copy of the novel idea you're going to flesh out—your novel on the head of a pin.

This is as good a place as any to get another rule behind us.

> **Cardinal Rule #5:** Finish your novel before you make the first attempt to sell it.

Nobody is going to buy your first novel without knowing you can complete it. By definition, no would-be novelist is certain of that. So forget the tales about million-dollar first novels sold on the basis of an idea etched into the foil of a gum wrapper. Plant your fanny in a chair, and write your story from start to finish.

Start with the "nugget"—two or three sentences crammed with information. A nugget contains these elements.

**Your working title.** If you have one. If you don't, we'll develop that first thing in the next chapter. If you must skip ahead, do that now, but come back here after you've found your working title.

**Your category.** Two words, tops. Is your story a romance, comedy or romantic comedy? Is it a thriller, a crime thriller, a techno-thriller, a mystery, a fantasy, an action-adventure, a western, science fiction, a horror, a coming-of-age story or something else? What category would define your intended work? If you can't identify a category, look over the list in *Writer's Market*, or check out the genres, complete with best-seller lists, on the Internet (amazon.com).

Caution: Stick to one or two genres only, please. You ought not submit a romantic-sci-fi-crime-thriller-western unless you feel compelled to reveal yourself as an amateur. And an idiot besides.

**Your sketch of the novel.** Thirty-five to forty words that pack your entire story on their little backs.

Here's an example of the nugget I'm using to write the first novel in a military action series for the Berkeley Putnam Publishing Group:

### *Force Recon*

#### Action-Adventure

A Marine lieutenant's elite band fights a running battle against terrorists behind enemy lines—*in Canada*. French separatists trap Navy SEALs and Army Rangers, and Force Recon rescues the Americans and erases all evidence of a U.S. invasion.

Thirty-nine words, not counting the title and category. What's explicit in that very short story?
- **The heroic character**—a Marine lieutenant
- **The central issue of the story** (plot line, if you will), including
- **The heroic goal**—to punish terrorists and rescue other elite forces before the United States is accused of invading Canada
- **The worthy adversary**—the terrorists, all of Canada, public opinion and (implied) elite teams of other services
- **Action**—explicit in the firefights and rescue
- **The ending**—Force Recon rescuing the Americans and erasing all evidence of an invasion

As a bonus, the 39 words include
- **A grabber**—fighting terrorists *and* rescuing SEALs and Rangers

- **A twist**—the United States invading *Canada*

Write a nugget based on your idea for a novel. Include all of these elements and more, if you wish.

### Some tips on writing your nugget

**Write as if telling a best friend** about a movie you have just seen.

**Don't worry about word count** the first time through. Just get it down. Address all the elements of a salable idea.

**Use present-tense,** specific verbs that describe the action as if it is happening in the here and now. In the example, *fights*, *trap*, *rescues* and *erases* were used.

**Use precise nouns.**

**Tighten.** Don't stop refining this until you get to 35 to 40 words. Fewer words means you're leaving out a possible grabber. More means you're not exercising the requisite discipline.

How about your own nugget? Got it done? Great. Now that it's dead solid perfect . . .

## STEP 4: TRY SHOOTING DOWN YOUR IDEA

Play the devil's advocate. Does your idea sound familiar? It couldn't be that you just saw the same plot dramatized on *The X-Files*, could it? Is your story a knockoff of the last novel you read? An item out of last night's news? If so, go back to step one and identify a new idea.

Later, if you feel a sudden urge to change your idea at any time, go right ahead. Modify your existing nugget statement right in the middle of your novel, or select a new one. Each time you change course, however, be sure to test it against reality.

Now let's have some fun with your nugget.

## STEP 5: POSITION YOUR IDEA WHERE YOU CAN SEE IT

Type or print your idea onto 3″ × 5″ cards. Carry one in the pocket of your blouse or shirt. Put one in the place where you'll be writing your novel. Put another on the visor of your car. Carry one in your planner. Keep this nugget before you as a reminder of your novel and the story you have committed to telling. I like to say that:

Once you have your snazzy new nugget on paper, you have, in effect, written the first draft of your novel.

A novel of only 40 words? Sounds bizarre on first reading, I admit. But think about it in this light: Now that you have narrowed the concept into a tight statement, the rest of this book is devoted to teaching you how to nurture and grow your seed novel of 40 words into a full-blown manuscript. The nugget will hold your focus and set the limits of the topic, keeping you on track until you write "The End."

# 2 INVENT THE FIRST CRITICAL PIECES OF YOUR NOVEL

**10 steps that will take your novel from a salable idea into the first stages of reality—building the Writer's Tool Kit**

> Not all popular novelists are good,
> but all good novelists are,
> sooner or later, popular.
>
> Dean Koontz

## STEP 1: CHOOSE A WORKING TITLE

A good title works magic on books and films. Somebody utters the title *Jaws* and the image in the mind of the listener is instantaneous, vivid and toothy. The power of that title comes not only from the work itself but also from the promotional machine that entrenched the title in the popular psyche.

Even without multimillion-dollar advertising behind it, a title from antiquity can strike a spark in the imagination: *Hamlet*, *Little Women*, *Oedipus Rex* or *Psycho*, for instance.

A grabber title can work wonders for your novel.

**It can keep you fired up** as you write the book. What could be more important than to sustain your passion until your novel is ready to share with the world?

**It can snag the attention of an agent or editor** when it heads your proposal package offering the completed novel to examine.

**It can sell your novel** to the book-buying public and to Hollywood filmmakers. In his book *How to Write Best-Selling Fiction* (Writer's

Digest Books), Dean Koontz says the five things that influence somebody to buy a book are (1) a proven author's name; (2) the subject matter of the novel; (3) the cover art; (4) the influence of the ad copy on the covers; (5) a quick reading of the first page.

You won't even have a prayer of snagging a potential buyer if he doesn't pick up the book and handle it. That's where your title comes in. A great title inspires great cover art, and together, the two can induce an impulse buyer to pick up your novel from the book table and peruse that first page.

Test your title against reality.

### Is your working title short and snappy?

As a rule, snappy titles give a book commercial appeal. Editors, reviewers, sellers and critics prefer a short handle when talking about your novel. Also, short titles fit best on a book's spine.

Naturally every consideration has its exception. *Midnight in the Garden of Good and Evil* isn't short and doesn't snap. Ditto: *Snow Falling on Cedars* and *The Horse Whisperer*, *How Stella Got Her Groove Back* and *The Bridges of Madison County*. But don't we wish those were our titles, novels and royalty payments?

### Does your title position your book?

It should be clear to editors, agents, marketing people, booksellers and book buyers what category your book fits or what topic you'll be addressing. *The Six-Gun Kid* suggests one thing and *A Virtuous Woman* something else again.

Don't use obscure or made-up words. Generally speaking, a title such as *Exsanguination* would be inferior to *Bloodletting* by this criterion, and it ought to be plain that the topic has to do with either emergency medicine or murder or both. Of course, if V.C. Andrews, Jackie Collins, Maya Angelou, Dean Koontz, Stephen King, Robin Cook, Patricia Cornwell or any one of a dozen famous authors puts out the title *Exsanguination*, you can almost envision the topic (and blockbuster sales).

But first novelists have a harder time using obscure words. You should stick to phrases that don't have to be explained in the course of a story. Again, *Midnight in the Garden of Good and Evil*, which has little to do with gardening, fails this test. Wish it were my failure.

Related to this consideration is the next one.

### Does your title use foreign words or dated references?

A first novelist who wants to sell commercial fiction can't afford to give editors the impression that the book is either too literary or too technical. I would suggest leaving dates off the title unless you've got another *1984* on your hands.

### Does your title lend itself to cover artwork?

Read the following new and old titles, and make note of all the possible cover art imagery that pops into your head.

*Jaws* (teeth)

*Cold Mountain* (Civil War carnage)

*White Fang* (more teeth)

*A Christmas Carol* (ghosts, chains)

*Interview With the Vampire* (still more teeth)

What artwork does your title inspire and envision? Teeth might be good. Finally, remember this about good titles . . .

### A good title is what your publisher says it is.

Many best-selling authors have title approval in their contracts. Experts and celebrities can capitalize on their power to insist on titles for their books. All you have is the power of persuasion.

Publishing companies know more than you about selling books. If they insist on a title change, give in.

### Sources of titles

**Your novel's content**—the first and foremost source. Let's face it, infringement aside, you couldn't get away with calling your novel *Jaws IX* if it had nothing to do with sharks. When readers see the word *Jaws*, they expect swimmers sinking into clouds of red in the sea—the title would never fly on a western.

Begin with a central phrase or issue within the novel, a noun or verb with some grabbing power. Then toy with it till something hits you between the eyes.

Dean Koontz works a wonderful illustration of ragging on title possibilities in *How to Write Best-Selling Fiction*, taking the concept of "dragon" and massaging it until he comes up with the title *Soft Come the Dragons*. Lack of space prevents showing his discussion here, but I encourage you to find Koontz's book in the library and check it out.

**Scripture,** as from a single church bulletin one recent Sunday—*Your Brother's Wife, Half My Kingdom, John the Beheaded, By the Sword, Prophecy at Bethel, The King's Sanctuary, Benediction.*

**Plays,** as in Shakespeare's *Much Ado About Nothing*—*John the Bastard, The Constable of Dogberry, Lady Disdain, The Windy Side of Care, Cry Mercy, Dance of the Stars, Life in the Death of a Marriage, Time Goes on Crutches, Kill Claudio.*

**Quotations**—*The Opposite of Love, Falseface, Presumption of Guilt, Walking in Armor, The Greyest Puritan, Satan's Miracle, Utter Silence, A Poverty of Wit.*

**Everywhere else**—From a snack package: *Dangerously Cheesy*; the newspaper: *Standoff*; a booklet on fly-fishing: *Blood Knot*; an almanac: *The 96th Thesis.*

A good title can be found anywhere. The most important thing you can do is keep your eyes and ears open to the possibilities and write a wonderful title when it presents itself to you.

Got a title of your own yet? Before you submit a manuscript, check the title in a directory of books in print. You wouldn't want to submit a title that Dick Francis has already used, would you?

Let's have some fun with all the pieces you've created so far.

## STEP 2: PLAY GOD WITH YOUR NOVEL

Better yet, go over God's head and play publisher. Now in keeping with cardinal rule number three—"Begin with the end in mind"—you manufacture an image of the finished product. This involves two phases, the tangible and the intangible. First some intangibles.

### Visualize the completed novel

Just as the world-class marathoner closes her eyes and imagines breaking the tape ahead of a field of runners, imagine what your book will look like when it's published. Either in your head or in person, travel to a bookstore and find the spot where your book will be shelved. If you want to begin by seeing your novel displayed by the dozens in the storefront window, fine. If you picture it on a stand-alone display rack, envision that. If you'd like to see it as the number eight best-seller alongside Patricia Cornwell, by all means, see it. In fact, feel free to go all the way. Imagine it as number one, an Oprah's Book Club selection held up and recommended to a national television audience. In your mind you're a publisher now, so anything is possible.

Pick up a novel by your favorite author, particularly the writer you want to emulate in sales and talent. Get the heft of the book. Check the number of pages. Read the ad copy, review snippets and quotes. Is this the kind of book you want published? Great.

While you're in the bookstore anyhow, find a book that represents the kind of cover art and type you want to see on your own book. Refer to your *Writer's Market* and decide which publisher will pay you for the right to edit, print and distribute your novel. Check directories and find the agent who will represent your work.

Heck, as long as you're in a fantasy land anyhow, pick out a dozen or so cities for your national tour to promote the book. Visualize being in every one of them. Have an imaginary cocktail in New York and send the tab to your fantasy publisher.

Finally, visualize the film that will be created from your novel. Cast the movie if you wish. Go ahead, dare to dream in Technicolor and without guilt. For this is not a mindless exercise in daydreaming. No, it's a step in the process of writing a novel. Visualizing gives focus to your project, a vision of success as you define it.

Just remember one thing: A marathoner can visualize herself into the retirement home if she wants to, but she can never actually *win* a race until she takes some tangible, physical steps—more than twenty-six miles worth of steps in fact.

So let's get started.

### Create a physical prototype of your novel

In this phase of step two, you awaken from your dream and craft a tangible book—the prototype of your novel. You can take this exercise to any degree of elaboration you wish.

- **Choose a book the size and shape** of the finished novel you have already visualized—something in your own book stacks.
- **Select paper** to use as a dust jacket.

- **Clip some magazine art** or draw the freehand image that will appear on your cover.
- **Add type.** Draw the title by hand, if you wish. Put your name on the cover as well. If you're feeling frisky, put these elements on the spine of the book and add a quote from somebody of the stature of John Grisham. Now affix the dust jacket to the book.
- **Display your prototype** in an area where you can see it as you write—right next to that nugget you've already written. *Voilà!* You now have a tangible motivator that can inspire you to keep writing when you're feeling lazy.

## STEP 3: INVEST IN SOME SIMPLE SUPPLIES FOR YOUR WRITER'S TOOL KIT

Your Writer's Tool Kit can save you hours of time wasted in duplication of effort and flat-out boneheaded mistakes. Unlike the prototype cover you created in step two, this is no mere self-motivation gimmick. The writer's kit is an indispensable invention.

### *Essential components of your Writer's Tool Kit*
- one pocket folder (either legal or regular size will do)
- one file folder (same size as your pocket folder)
- one writing tablet (matched in size to your pocket folder)
- one 100-count packet of $3'' \times 5''$ cards
- one 100-count packet of $5'' \times 8''$ cards
- transparent tape (the kind you can write on is best)
- a pen or pencil

One optional component I often rely on is a portable audiocassette recorder. Use it to take oral notes should an idea strike you while you're driving and unable to jot a memo to yourself. It comes in handy when you're struck by a barrage of simultaneous ideas—you can put thoughts on tape faster than you can write them. Later you can play back your thoughts and make written notes.

## STEP 4: COLLECT A GALLERY OF CHARACTERS

Time for a little fun using a trick I learned from my friend, novelist Karl Largent. Untie that bundle of old magazines in the garage, and launch your own character hunt. Clip and rip, gathering bodies and faces to use in casting your novel. Look for photographs of the famous, the near famous and the unknown model whose portrait is used to sell everything from eye shadow to nasal hair clippers.

When you go to the doctor, dentist, barber or hairdresser, page through the magazines. Should you run across a character with character—any age, gender or race—do one of two things: Either run to the newsstand and buy that issue of the magazine so you can collect the character for your gallery, or rip the heart from the magazine right there in the waiting room. Your decision is between you, your conscience and your hairdresser.

Gather up the family photo albums and find the most interesting faces there. Drag out the high school yearbook. Collecting people you know lets you borrow personality traits as well as physical ones.

Store the pictures of possible characters in a box or a drawer. When a character enters your novel, transfer a picture to a pocket folder of your writer's kit, creating a gallery of characters.

This character gallery simplifies the strain on your imagination when you want to create a word picture of your heroine. You pull a photo from the folder pocket and apply a stick-on label with her name. Then, rather than conjuring her features from the ether, you refer to the picture and tell what you see there. I recommend plastering the walls of your writing area with characters from your novel.

> **Bonus Idea:** Use this same technique to collect settings for your novel (*National Geographic*), fashions (*GQ*, *Vogue*) and so on.

Three cautions in casting your novel.

**Caution one:** Don't collect only the beautiful. Gather people with glasses as well as contact lenses. Find all shades of skin and hair color. Look for the fat, the thin, the smooth, the rough. Find men with beards and women with mustaches. Search out warts, triple chins, crooked teeth, bald heads and wild hairs. In short, create a realistic world of characters. The novel packed with nothing but pretty people is too much to be believed.

**Caution two:** You may find it helpful to use photos of the famous and familiar, but don't identify them. Don't say your character has "Paul

Newman eyes." Give your hero an original persona. Along with this goes the warning to avoid describing Aunt Bertha right down to the identifying "Born to raise hell" tattoo across her nose. You wouldn't want to hurt Aunt Bertha's feelings—or to have her hurt yours.

Caution three: Don't get hung up on collecting characters. Sure, it's a fun activity, but it won't get your novel written. Keep moving.

## STEP 5: CREATE A DIRECTORY OF CHARACTER NAMES

Naming characters is fun—*except* when you're all wrapped up in writing a hot scene and a new character crashes the story. You won't want to interrupt your momentum to invent a name. Better to have a list of names filed away in your Writer's Tool Kit. Here's how to build your own ready-to-use name directory.

### 1. Collect some interesting last names

- **Divide a sheet of paper** from the pad you bought for your writer's kit into three columns as shown in figure one.
- **Open a telephone directory** to the *A* listings.
- **Copy some interesting last names** into the first column of your name directory. I suggest you collect three to five last names that begin with *A*.

| Name Directory | | |
|---|---|---|
| Last Names | First Names of Men | First Names of Women |
|  |  |  |
|  |  |  |

Fig. 1. Name directory

- **Do the same** for listings from *B* to *Z*. Don't worry if you have trouble finding names that begin with *Q*, *U*, *X* and *Z*. You may get only one or two. No problem. Just go on to the next letter.

### 2. Collect some interesting first names

Pick any page in the phone book, and write down the best male and female first names you find. Fill the last two columns of your directory with these names. Caution: Do *not* put the real first names of people alongside their real last names.

When it comes time to build some names for your heroic characters, choose a last name you like from the directory. Then choose a first name that goes with it. Say the full name aloud to see if it sounds all right. If you want to, choose a middle name from the list. Each time you select a name and write it onto a character card—which we'll create soon— cross it off the worksheet so you won't use it again.

When you need a name for antiheroic characters, perform the same drill as before with a negative bent. What would you call the evil step-mothers of your stories?

Don't get silly here. Naming a bully Spike is too much. A wicked woman doesn't have to be called Cruella for us to understand her nature. Names like those are for the cartoons and comics. Your job as novelist will be to round out a character by weaving a rich texture of behavior rather than simple labels. Look what Thomas Harris did with the heroic name Hannibal in *The Silence of the Lambs*.

The minute you feel yourself choosing a name that automatically seems bad or good to you, ask whether it's because of somebody you know. Chances are, you'll be creating a snobbish character named Cynthia because of a Cynthia you knew but did not like. Bad idea. Give her a different name.

## A final checklist for your name directory

Run each name past this checklist before you transfer it from your name directory to a character card.

√ **Don't use names of real people,** even if you're trying to be kind to your friends. You might insult somebody who misreads your intended compliment. What's more, people who wish to keep their lives private don't like reading stories about them-selves, even true and complimentary ones.

√ **Don't use names that sound like the names of real people** or somebody else's characters. Sorry, you can't get around the first "don't" by moving a few letters around in the name. If you insulted a character named Clillary Hinton, we'd know.

√ **Don't use names that might be confused with famous fictional characters, either.** Clark Kent would be a lousy name for one of your characters, and you could be sued for using it. Worse, you'd be guilty of a far more heinous crime: utter lack of originality.

√ **Don't use names that sound alike.** This is a "don't" that has several possibilities to consider:

- **Avoid names that begin with the same letter.** I once wrote a novel using characters named Darwin, Dewey and Del. Too confusing, so I changed names.
- **Avoid names that can be both masculine and feminine.** Eliminate Pat, Terry, Robin and Bobby unless your story intentionally confuses the identity to create a twist.
- **Be wary of names that could be first and last names.** Grant or Tyler or James or Kelly or Chase or Terry— each name could be last or first.
- **Don't overuse alliteration,** that is, first and last names that begin with the same letter. Bobby Burns, Todd Trotter and Kay Kaufman in the same story? Too much.
- **Don't use names** that sound like half the people in the phone book. Mary Jones? Bill Johnson? Nuh-uh. Try to be a little creative. And never use Jim Smith—it's my name, and way too common already.
- **And don't use names that rhyme** in the same story—Bill, Gil, Jill, Lil, Phil and Zill (Zill?).

√ **Be wary of long names.** Imagine a heroic character by the name of Degaetanis. You'd get exhausted just typing a name like that a thousand times.

That's not to say you can't use long names. You may write a novel with Russians in it. To keep it realistic, you'll *need* confusing names.

Besides, you may know a trick to get around a difficult name. You can shorten it to a nickname. And yes, you can use the global change feature of your software program to change every instance of the shorthand *Deg* to *Degaetanis*. (When performing the global change, don't forget the word space that follows *Deg* or you'll have to go back to ferret out and correct words such as *degree* and *degrade* that got changed to *Degaetanisree* and *Degaetanisrade*—been there, done that.)

√ **Be conscious of names ending in s.** This can cause awkward punctuation when you want to show possession. Suppose your heroic character is Iris James. Whatever she possesses is Iris's. When two or more members of her family appear in a scene, they are the Jameses. Their house is the Jameses'—enough to make you avoid such names altogether.

√ **Don't be too cute.** *Doris B. Goode?* Maybe in a kid's storybook, but nowhere else.

√ **Don't use a name twice.** Remember: Cross a name off your name directory when you transfer it to your character card.

## STEP 6: CREATE A CHARACTER PORTFOLIO FOR YOUR TOOL KIT

Time to put names and faces together. The people who will act out the idea you've refined into your nugget are your characters, of course. And anybody who's ever read a tale or seen a movie or television show knows that not all characters have equal stature in these stories.

### *Characters in your portfolio come in three categories*

We'll discuss each category in greater detail later. For now all you need to know is the headline about each.

**Master characters** drive the story. By their personalities, behavior and decisions, they dictate the action, timing, direction and pace of your novel. They are the

- heroic character (protagonist)
- heroic character's adversary (antagonist)
- heroic character's love interest (love interest)

They are the Clark Kent, Lex Luthor and Lois Lane of your novel. You ought to give them faces and personalities as striking as their responsibilities in carrying your novel on their backs.

> **Cardinal Rule #6:** At the minimum, you should have three master characters for your novel. At the maximum, you should have three.

To review the reasons for such dogmatic declarations, refer to "The Essential Elements of a Salable Novel" in chapter one.

**Major characters** play a substantial role in *helping* master characters drive the story. They are Perry White and Jimmy Olsen to your Lois and Clark. They make decisions within the story context, but they seldom dictate the outcome of important events. Only master characters do that in salable novels, and don't you forget it. Select unique pictures for these characters as well.

**Minor characters** are all your extras. They're the walk-ons, the cab-drivers, the relatives of your master and major characters. Mind, these are not stereotypes. They have distinctive personalities even if they're not rounded as fully as the important players.

With a bit of luck and a lot of craft on your part, all your master and major characters will assume lives of their own. Readers love this type of character better than any artificial, two-dimensional stereotype. In fact, such characters can grow unruly as their natures develop throughout their story. What's more, as the cast fills out, you might get confused by the number of new acquaintances alone. Finally, a mountain of personal detail shapes your characters throughout the novel, and you can be overcome by the sheer mass of your creation.

That's why you need a character portfolio in your writer's kit. Some writers keep track of characters in a concordance, a list of characters with columns for various details, such as color of eyes, age and other demographics. Such a concordance works fine when you're recording driver's license data (eyes, hair color, height, weight) but doesn't allow enough space for expanding detail.

Other writers write complete dossiers on their characters. They record exhaustive background material that helps the writer construct a lush context for telling a story realistically.

The character portfolio falls between these extremes. It gives you a means to record tidbits of demographic data *and* to develop selected concepts in some depth—but not too much. Perhaps this is the best feature of the portfolio. It forces you to set priorities and limit the size of the biographies you write on each character.

If that's not the best feature of the portfolio, this is: The character portfolio puts a character's personal detail, large and small, at the tip of your finger—literally.

## *Building the character portfolio*
### Assemble the pieces
From your batch of supplies, you'll need the
- packet of 5″ × 8″ cards
- packet of 3″ × 5″ cards
- file folder
- transparent tape—with a finish you can write on

### Create 5″ × 8″ character cards
You'll use these cards for both your master and major characters. Here's a picture of such a card, prepared using a computer illustration program and generated by a high-quality printer.

| Character | ☐ Master ☐ Major Role/Title: | |
|---|---|---|
| Pertinent Bio | Physical | Distinctive Language |
| | Hair_____ Eyes_____ Nose_____ Mouth_____ Hands_____ Striking Features | |
| Goal/Motivation | – Fatal Flaw | |
| 1. _____ 2. _____ 3. _____ | + Saving Grace | |
| Name: | ″    ″ | Age: (    ) |

*Fig. 2. Character card (5″ × 8″) for master and major characters*

Yours doesn't have to be so elaborate. The important point is that you allow room for each of the regions on the card. You can label your cards in pen and write the information in pencil. Or you can forget about the headings altogether and write data in specified regions, referring to a master card as a legend. You decide how.

If you insist on using space-age technology, here are a couple ideas to create cards quickly and easily:

- **Enlarge the illustration above** on a photocopy machine and keep enlarging until you have a master to print to size on cards.
- **Create a template of the card** in your word processing program. Then you can either complete cards in your computer and print them or print cards with headings and complete them by hand. No matter how you do this, you'll end up adding some information by hand anyhow.
- **With ruled cards, turn them upside down** before printing headings. This will put the red rule and wide margin at the bottom of the card. Later you'll be taping the tops of these cards down, overlapping one over the other. If you need to flip up a card to write on the back, the wide margin will then be at the top.
- **Prepare twelve to twenty cards now.** In step seven, we'll discuss filling in the space under the headings.

| **Minor Character** Role/Title: | | |
|---|---|---|
| Hair: <br> Eyes: <br> Size: | Striking Feature: | Distinctive Language: |
| Connection to Master Characters: | | |
| Goal/Motivation: | | |
| Name:     "          "     Age:    (        ) | | |

*Fig. 3. Character Card (3" × 5") for minor characters*

### Create 3" × 5" character cards

These are for your minor characters. (See figure three above.)

Prepare twenty to thirty cards now.

## STEP 7: SKETCH OUT AT LEAST
## THREE MASTER CHARACTERS

Your master characters must sell your novel every bit as much as your sizzling plot and intriguing synopsis must. That's why we're going to spend so much time with them in this step.

Notice two qualities about master characters as I've defined them so far. First, by having only three people to know well, you simplify the task of knowing them in depth. Second, observe the terms I use in the discussion: *heroic character* rather than *protagonist*, which is something of a clinical word; *heroic character's adversary* instead of *antagonist*; and *heroic character's love interest*. The discussion of master characters is couched in terms of the heroic character alone. Here's why:

> **Cardinal Rule #7:** Your novel plays out in relation to the world of your heroic character. If an action, setting or other character does not relate to the heroic character—either as a cause or an effect—odds are, that action, setting or character doesn't belong in the novel.

If you focus on your heroic character's universe and derive your story from it as a starting point, enlarge it, dramatize it and follow it consistently to the ending, the job of writing your novel is simplified. What's more important, your final manuscript will have unity, coherence and all those other characteristics you barely remember from your literature classes. Best of all, you will have achieved them without ever thinking about them.

This notion is so important, I've written a corollary to rule seven:

Enough philosophy for now. Let's fill in some of the blanks on your master character cards, beginning with the heroic characters.

> **Cardinal Rule #8:** Think of your novel in terms of a heroic character's universe clashing with his adversary's universe and you will have distilled the business of writing a novel to its essence.

## *How to complete a master character card*
### Fill in the bottom line

Remember: If you're using ruled cards, the red line and wide margin becomes the bottom of the card.

**Name.** Write the heroic character's full name and initials here. If you haven't chosen a name for her, refer to your name directory in the pocket of your Writer's Tool Kit. Give her a name now.

" ". Between the quote marks, insert all the nicknames you have decided to use. If nicknames crop up later, you can add them.

**Age.** As they say in Canada, self-explanatory, eh?

( ). Should you base a novel's character on a real person, write the name in here to remind yourself of the connection. Caution: Write this name in pencil so you can erase it later to save yourself embarrassment—and by all means, do not identify the person by a description, title or name that risks getting you sued for libel. I confess that I once used a person I disliked as an inspiration to write a graphic scene. I directed a genetically engineered monster to devour him alive. Aside from revealing myself to you as perverse, I'm telling you it's sometimes useful when writing an emotional scene to tap into actual emotions you have experienced. And I repeat, the purpose of this device is to create a mood, not to ridicule or debase a person.

### Fill in the top line

**Master.** Check this box on the card for each of the three master characters. You know which box you'll check later, when you're completing cards for major characters, right?

**Role/Title.** Write "Heroic Character," for example, and her occupation or role in the story: CEO, helicopter pilot, drifter, supermodel, supermom.

### Complete the "Physical" section

If you haven't already decided on the master character's appearance, do so now. Refer to your character gallery in the writer's kit and pick the pictures of her to display on the wall. If you've decided to base this character on the name in parentheses on the bottom line, visualize her. You'll notice the character card doesn't allow a space to indicate either gender or race. We'll just assume you can keep track of those things either in your head or by referring to the photo gallery. As for the rest, you fill out these blanks so your character's characteristics don't change by accident midway through your novel.

**Hair.** Specify color and length at least; texture, shine and thickness if you must. Oh, and don't make every woman in your story a blonde.

**Eyes, nose, mouth, hands.** You can do this without prompts.

**Striking features.** Think about it. Everybody is memorable in some physical respect—either size, beauty, hideousness or one of the features already listed on the card. Here you note the character's signature features, two, tops. This feature is the one most likely to draw attention in the novel and become a tag by which a reader will identify the character. Quasimodo had his hunched back, and in Tom Robbins's novel *Even Cowgirls Get the Blues*, Sissy Hankshaw had enormous thumbs. A striking attribute allows you to create striking imagery, but, far more important is that:

> Within the story a character reacts to his striking feature in one or more ways, and other characters react in various differing ways, allowing you to characterize.

Quasimodo's hunchback made him a recluse so he could avoid being mocked, but Sissy Hankshaw idolized her oversized thumbs and exploited them all her life. Other characters in those tales reveal their natures—cruel, curious, kind and the like—in the ways they react to the hunchback and the thumbs.

You needn't create extremes to be effective with a striking feature. And you ought not create bizarre physical appendages for everybody in your novel. Your job is to develop believable personalities in your novel, to make characters come alive. A physical oddity alone will not carry such heavy and valuable freight for you. What works in the cartoons won't work in your novel.

**Rule of Thumb:** Generally, you will develop all master and most major characters well enough so you will not need to rely on a single physical tag to identify them to readers. Such a tag might be more useful in minor characters, which are not so rounded.

Later we'll discuss how to use the raw entries in this segment of the card in your novel.

## Write a brief "Pertinent Bio"

I know, you're grinding your teeth at the lack of space to write a bio. How can I be so inconsiderate as to expect you to cram an exciting life into the space of the front and back of a business card? Hey, go ahead and vent your spleen. You're going to appreciate this inconvenience later. What I'm doing is preventing you from a detour capable of distracting you from writing your novel. Don't write long biographical backgrounds. Period.

I don't care that Gustave Flaubert might have written a thousand pages creating a family tree and childhood history for Madame Bovary before he ever named a novel for her. Don't do it.

Some would argue that you should know your character better than your family. When you write your novel, they say, you can recall facts from a lengthy bio to attain a superior level of realism.

I say, Baloney! The majority of writers, after they have invested so much energy in creating a complete new life, will be compelled to transfer entire biographical files into their novels. They'll have a thousand valid reasons for this compulsion: gotta make the word count; gotta get the background in; gotta understand where the character's coming from.

Baloney again. One sure way to make your novel boring is to include all the junk you've labored over before starting your manuscript. To paraphrase the novelist Elmore Leonard, don't write the stuff that readers skip. To which I add, there's a reason that the only customers for biographical tomes such as *Who's Who* are libraries and the people who are in them. Let me state this in the form of

> **Cardinal Rule #9:** Never get sidetracked on issues such as exhaustive biographical sketches and detailed physical settings. Do all your important writing in your novel, not in preparation.

One of the great experiences in writing a novel is the sudden, unforeseen revelation to the novelist. You might experience that flash of insight that tosses all your preconceptions to the wind. The characters present new possibilities to you, and you react, redirecting the story. In such a case only two things can happen with voluminous background material, both of them bad: One, the stuff you labored over needs to be trashed; two (and worse yet), you feel hidebound by the effort you expended, and you forfeit a fresh idea to the work you've already invested in. This latter case is the bane of all writers, but especially inexperienced ones.

So, write brief, telegraphic—even incomplete—sketches, notes to yourself to use in fleshing out characters and settings in the novel.

An example out of my Force Recon series—actual notes from my character card bio on the heroic character, Lieutenant Joseph Swayne:

- The unit's leader. Tough, resourceful, persistent, capable of thinking under fire and acting coolly.

- Off-duty, a loner, relates poorly to most civilians, though he has a sharp wit. He's capable of warmth—and is utterly taken by an unlikely romantic interest, reporter Nina Chase.

- Once a wild, unfocused kid—his father was declared missing in action in Vietnam—he was raised by an uncle who made him toe the line.

- His grandfather, a U.S. senator, is opposed to his career, telling him that his father was lost because he didn't measure up, and that he possesses the same weaknesses.

- He suffers night sweats, fearing his grandfather is right, wondering if this mission will prove it.

Anything else I'll write into the novel.

Time for you to write brief sketches of your master characters. Put down what you know, even if it's only a few words. Later, more ideas will reveal themselves to you. You can work the new biographical data right into the manuscript and make a notation in the bio section. This card is a working document, one you can scribble on at any time, a place to record spontaneous notes about story elements you must remember for the sake of consistency.

If you already know your master characters' backgrounds and the directions of their lives in the course of your story in some detail, you may require more room. Use the back of the card (see, there is quite a lot of space, after all).

### Note the "Distinctive Language" segment of the card

Let's talk about creating a distinctive identity for your master characters. In the world outside a novel, you can distinguish individuals, their behaviors and their emotions in a hundred different ways. You can spot the one-of-a-kind eyebrows of your lover in a crowd of thousands at the ball game. A wink, a wave, a way of walking. One glimpse of these mannerisms and you know a friend's disposition.

You don't need an omniscient narrator standing at your shoulder whispering in your ear, "Your husband is angry with you for being so late." You can see that well enough by the way he's using the ten-inch flame of a butane torch to light the candles on your intimate anniversary dinner table. Actions and imagery characterize your characters. In the best writing, actions and imagery are so distinctive a reader can identify a character's emotions without the author pointing them out in so many words, as in, "He was angry."

Speaking of words. The utterance of a sigh, a guttural sound, the choice of a word, a lilt in the voice—these speech mannerisms can be effective in creating a distinctive identity. Given time to reflect, you know very well you could identify at least one pet phrase for everybody you know. What does your boss unfailingly say when she's giving one of those things-are-going-to-have-to-change-around-here speeches? Does she open with, "People?" intoning the word like a question? Or does she just growl, "I've got some bad news and some terrible news"? When handled well, a reader will know who's speaking in your novel even if the author doesn't attribute every line of dialogue.

At this point of setting the stage for your novel, you may not know the individual vocabularies and speech patterns of your characters. No problem. Use this segment of the character card to record the peculiarities that identify them when they speak.

For instance, in the Force Recon series, one member of the unit, Delmont Potts, is a huge, garrulous man, easygoing and friendly, given to uttering colorful, ironic phrases just this side of clichés. To one of his mates decked out in battle dress and camouflage, Potts says: "Ain't you a sight? Pretty as a speckled dog in the shade."

Each time a character like Potts distinguishes himself, annotate the

"Distinctive Language" region of that character's card with the word, expression or vocal mannerism. As the novel progresses, you can refer to his card each time that character gets involved in a scene so you can remain true to a character and perhaps even enrich his characterization. At a minimum you will reduce the number of inconsistencies that can make you look like an amateur.

The distinctive language tool in your writer's kit comes with its own set of cautions.

### Distinctive language dos and don'ts

**Don't write dialects.** Readers don't like dialects, and editors hate them. Reasons enough to avoid writing them. Not to mention the possibilities of offending a racial or social minority. Better to hint at a dialect in the vocabulary and sentence construction.

For example: "Whatchoo gunna do 'bout it, mistuh?" is far inferior to "What are you gonna do about it, mister?" in which only one word is nonstandard English. Let the reader supply her own interpretation of slurring, drawling, singsong speech patterns instead of trying to re-create them on paper. For a great example, see Kaye Gibbons's *Ellen Foster* to see how a southern child's voice is handled.

**Don't borrow speech patterns from television.** Leave expressions such as "I don't think so" to *Home Improvement* and "He is so not considerate" to *Friends*. If your characters talk like the central foursome on *Seinfeld*, every editor and agent in America will recognize your lack of originality. Besides, pet phrases that get into the mainstream from pop culture are usually short-lived. Why date your book with obnoxious Wayne and Garth constructions such as: "I want broccoli for dessert. Not!"

**Don't overuse an identification tag.** In one of my novels, I found during the revision process that a major character was using *acourse* (for *of course*) every other line. The use of dialect aside, the device began to stink after the first hundred uses or so.

**Don't strain** over creating distinctive speech. If you press too hard, it will show in obvious, repetitive expressions.

**Do let your talent develop naturally.** Distinguishing characters with speech tags will improve as you exercise this skill. Eventually your best results will prove to be subtle, even understated. These will be your most memorable characters.

## Identify "Goal/Motivation," "Fatal Flaw" and "Saving Grace"

Finally, the central issues of writing a novel.

**Goal/Motivation.** Here you record the most critical goals and urgent motivations of your heroic character. If you need clarification, a goal is an objective, tangible or otherwise, that a character wants to achieve. A motivation is a reason for wanting that goal—greed, love, duty, ambition and so on. I try to round out a character by enumerating three types of goals in this space.

**Career or idealistic personal goals.** These things a character seeks to fulfill a higher call. For instance, in the pilot novel of the Force Recon series, Lieutenant Swayne's primary goal is to rescue the Commandant of the Marine Corps, who's been snatched by terrorists. Swayne's motivation is duty to mission and the Corps. This goal conflicts with the goals of the terrorists and becomes the central story line.

**Selfish goals.** Everybody has self-interests and base instincts. This category addresses those. Swayne's secondary goal is to prove his grandfather wrong in thinking that the lieutenant doesn't have what it takes to be a Force Recon Marine. Swayne is also motivated by a need to exorcise the demons of self-doubt on that very issue.

**Romantic or sexual goals.** This category addresses both the animal urges and love interests of characters. Swayne's goal here is to romance investigative reporter Nina Chase, who's trying to build her own career by ruining his. Swayne doesn't even know why he's drawn to this woman. All he knows is that he'd be willing to give up even his career if he could win her.

However you handle goals and motivations, start by asking: What does my character stand for? What does he want? What is he against? Why? You'll want to give these questions some thought, for they are important enough to generate the next two cardinal rules:

> **Cardinal Rule #10:** A heroic character's goals and motivations cannot lead to trivial pursuits. Master characters must be given to furious passions, driving forces, lifetime ambitions and fundamental values. A character must be willing to risk all, even life, for such things.

Earlier I talked about the universe of the heroic character clashing with the universe of her adversary. Here is where you clarify and document the expression of that collision. Whatever the heroic character is for, the heroic character's adversary is against. What the heroine wants, the antiheroine tries to steal.

> **Cardinal Rule #11:** The central conflict in a novel arises from the powerful, usually violent struggle between the opposing goals and motivations of the heroic character and his adversary.

The best way to examine these cardinal rules is to demonstrate them with examples. I use *Jaws* and *Jurassic Park* quite often, not because they're the greatest stories ever told but because you have likely seen the films even if you haven't read the books.

In *Jaws* the heroic character (the sheriff of Amity) risks his reputation and his life to maintain the safety of his community and family by hunting down and killing the shark whose goals, though never enumerated, are clearly terrorist. If you want to argue for the creation of three heroic characters who team up against the shark, fine. Although multiple heroes don't always work, this story might be one notable exception, perhaps because although the trio share their goal, each has a different motivation. The sheriff's is his devotion to duty; the scientist seeks both data and thrills; and the *Orca*'s captain, Quint, is borderline psychotic. It makes for great conflict as the men clash with each other as well as with the shark.

In *Jurassic Park* John Hammond is driven to create the world's most elite theme park, one populated with living dinosaurs. This goal clashes with the goals of his investors, the good sense of his scientific advisers, his competitors and the very laws of nature itself. Now *that's* a titanic conflict. What you might find odd is that this central character's goal drives the film, although you may not classify him as a master character in the sense I've defined one. I'd argue that, unwitting though he may seem, Hammond is the heroic characters' adversary. He's the guy, after all, who drags the heroic characters out of the badlands of Montana and throws them into conflict with his creations, right?

By the way, I haven't said who the heroic character is because here's a story in which, in the film version, an obvious penchant for political correctness gave us dual heroic characters: paleontologist Alan Grant and paleobotanist Ellie Sattler. If it weren't for those nasty raptors stealing and solidifying the film, you'd notice the contrivance, a kind of "You be the hero for a while" approach followed every few minutes by "OK, enough for you—now it's my turn to be the heroine." Here's a buddy picture that doesn't work the way buddy pictures are supposed to, and, in my opinion, doesn't work at all, no matter how much I love the story.

You ought to be able to indicate the goals and motivations of each of your master characters by now. So do so.

**Fatal flaws and saving graces.** When you first tested your novel idea against reality, you read about these concepts. Here I'll elevate them to the level of a cardinal rule:

> **Cardinal Rule #12:** Even the most heroic character is somehow flawed, often seriously, and the nastiest villain has some saving grace, no matter how small.

You could cite several reasons for creating characters according to this rule. In fact, here are two.

**Realism.** Flawed heroes and villains with at least one redemptive quality seem more realistic—more human (in cases of human characters).

**Dramatic tension** is increased in any instance when the heroic character can be defeated unless she overcomes her flaws. Same for a villain who cannot overcome his saving grace.

Let's examine the chart on the following page and some of the cast in *Jaws*, trying to pinpoint fatal flaws and saving graces.

*Jaws*

| Character | Fatal Flaw | Saving Grace |
|-----------|-----------|--------------|
| Shark | Too stupid to realize it could hide in the sea. | It's just a creature doing what creatures do. |
| Sheriff | So ill-equipped for shark hunting he could die. | He's *so* determined and devoted to duty. |
| Scientist | Thrill and fame seeking could get him killed. | Competence and bravery. |
| *Orca's* captain | Obsession with killing that shark drives him to take unacceptable risks. | He's not a bad guy— and he *did* have that awful WWII experience. |

And so on. Time for you to complete as much of your master character cards as you can and move on to major characters.

## STEP 8: SKETCH OUT THE MAJOR CHARACTERS YOU ALREADY KNOW

This is simple stuff. Using one of the same cards, in the top line, check "Major" instead of "Master," and perform the same operations you did in the previous step.

Granted, you may not have given much thought to major characters. No problem. If you know your heroic character will have to deal with two former boyfriends as well as her current romance, give them names and faces and put the partially filled cards in a stack. Family, co-workers, bosses and friends will be major characters in your novels. Very soon we'll place all your cards into a fingertip arrangement that allows you to update and expand character data as your novel develops. For now, bear in mind these few points.

### Considerations for major characters

In the "Pertinent Bio" section, tell how these characters will interact with master characters. And they *must* interact. Otherwise, they're crashing your novel without an invitation and floating around like space dust without a purpose. Jot a note here to remind yourself of the connection. It might be "Doting father of the heroine—meddles in all her relationships" or "Hero's best friend who becomes an unwitting accessory to his adversary by . . ." Something like that.

Under "Goal/Motivation," "Fatal Flaw" and "Saving Grace," write something meaningful. Give each character a clear purpose. Naturally, you, the author, have a purpose for inserting a character into a scene. It might be as contrived as inventing a drop-in friend so you can write dialogue instead of having your heroic character musing and fuming inside his own head about being arrested. But if you want *all* your characters to come alive on the page, you must give them reasons to live on their own. For instance, the friend isn't an idle drop-in, after all; he's broke and wants to borrow money. The heroic character refuses, revealing that he was arrested for trespassing and had to put up a cash bond. The friend challenges this as an absurd excuse. They argue. The friend storms out. Scene over.

Notice what happened. The action focuses on the argument, which allows information about the arrest to be revealed and shows the worsening circumstances of the heroic character. This technique is far superior to one character spouting information to another.

> **Cardinal Rule #13:** Give major characters—and even minor characters—goals and motivations of their own. Permit them to have personal reasons for being in your novel rather than using them as set pieces for your convenience.

I warn you, if you don't give this notion of purposeful characters some high-quality thought, you'll end up with boring characters or find yourself resorting to stereotypes: the crotchety cop with a heart of mush, the sleazy playboy always getting his face slapped and the like.

Connect goals and motivations of major characters to those of the master characters. In life people play by looser rules than in novels. They don't have to clash or cooperate with each other and often don't care to. In novels, you must establish relationships, causes and effects. Things happen for reasons, and almost always because of either cooperative efforts or conflicts of interest. So, however tenuously you choose to execute this concept, connect.

You might expect the goals and motivation of a major character to coincide with the heroic character's because they're friends. Instead, as in the example above, they clash, making for a better story.

## STEP 9: SKETCH IN MINOR CHARACTERS

Fat chance. At this stage of your novel, chances are, you haven't met your minor characters. These are the extras, the walk-ons who drop in, drop out and often never reappear. In a murder mystery, they're the nameless handful of victims who, by their timely deaths, establish that a serial killer is on the loose. Eventually, master and major characters will hurl their courageous selves into harm's way, but a few of the little people have to die first.

They're also the surly cabdrivers, tough-talking prostitutes, pesky little sisters, snotty (or efficient) secretaries and occasional friends of other characters. When the credits roll at the end of a movie, they're the "Cop #1" and "Fat man in polka-dot pants."

Or, maybe they're even the original minor characters you create on your own instead of falling back on types.

You can fill in the various sections of the 3″ × 5″ minor character card as you please. And quite often you will not fill them out at all, other than to indicate on the bottom line something like "menacing drunk" in place of a name. You might limit the physical description to only one feature, which might not be striking, as I have defined striking above. The distinctive speech might be quite ordinary.

Here, briefly, are some additional hints.

### Considerations for minor characters

**Complete the "Connection"** section when you introduce the character. Tell how a minor character comes into contact with a master or major character and why. Should this minor character later assert her presence and demand a role as a major character, you'll have a bit of history to get you started on a 5″ × 8″ card for her.

**Do not overdescribe minor characters.** Don't allow them the same degree of detail reserved for major and master characters. Later, I'll debunk a good deal of the conventional wisdom about description altogether. For now, just remember to apply some descriptive scale appropriate to the importance of minor characters.

**Supply goals and motivations.** Yes, even for minor characters. This keeps you focused on the needs, wants and purposes of the player rather than your own utilitarian requirement to throw in a character just because your hero needs somebody to punch in the mouth. If the goals and motivations of minor characters are minor, don't worry about it. If a little brother's ambition in life is to grow up to be like his sister, no problem. If a taxi driver's only purpose is to collect one more fare before going off shift, what's the harm?

**Don't give short shrift to minor characters.** Yes, they are minor. But do not blow off the importance of creating distinctive characters down to the least important one in your book. If you want to examine the work of a master of this concept, reread *Lonesome Dove*, by Larry McMurtry. Every soul who appeared in that novel, if only for a sentence, seemed remarkable. Strive for that kind of mastery. Even if you fall short, you will be well on the road to creating memorable characters.

## *Assemble your character portfolio*

Affix the master and major character cards to your file folder:

- Open the file folder.
- Place one 5″ × 8″ card (labeled but not filled in) on the inside right-hand area of your file folder.
- Align the bottom edge of the card (the edge with the "Name" line or red-ruled margin) with the bottom edge of the folder. The left edge of the card should be about a quarter inch from the fold.
- Using a strip of transparent tape (of the type you can write on, remember?), affix the card to the file folder along the card's top edge. Don't let the tape extend beyond the card, either to the right or left. This strip of tape acts as a hinge so you can flip up the card and write on the back—now you know why you should flip the card head to toe to add character data.
- When you're finished with that first card, the folder will look like the illustration in figure four.
- Take a second card and overlap all of the first card except for the bottom half inch or so, barely covering the red rule, if you're using lined cards. Tape this card in place as before so you can read the "Name" line of the bottom card.

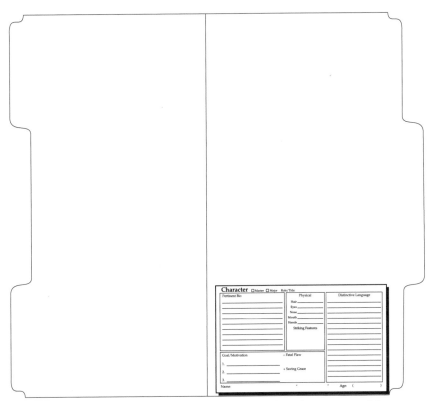

*Fig. 4. First character card (5″ × 8″) affixed in character portfolio*

- Count the number of cards you've already made entries on. As you continue taping down cards, you'll reserve room for these cards, arranging the master character cards at the top of the overlapping stack.
- Continue taping cards with the half-inch overlap that exposes the "Name" line of each card until it looks like figure five.

## How to use the "fingertip" character portfolio

As you write your novel, you will want to record or refer to a detailed bio or physical description from time to time. You place your fingertip on the "Name" line of that character and flip up all the cards above it. All is revealed. Should you introduce a new major character, point to

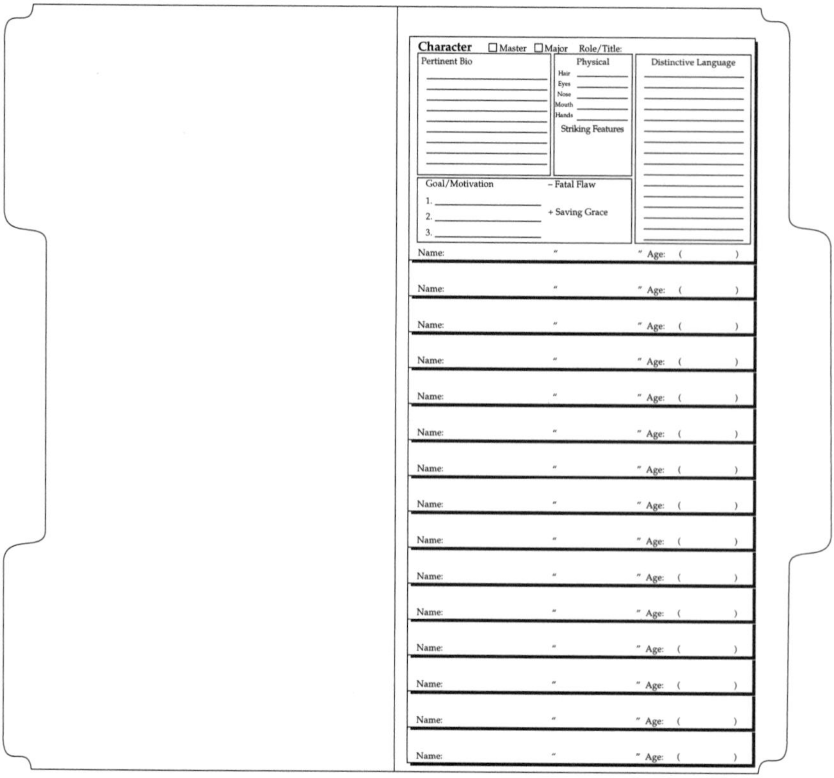

*Fig. 5. Character portfolio with 5″ × 8″ affixed*

and reveal the first available blank card and start entering pertinent data. When your character spouts an inventive word or phrase that is peculiar to her, flip to her card and record the signature remark under the "Distinctive Language" segment. Not exactly rocket science, eh?

### Affix the minor character cards

Same deal. Start at the bottom of the left side of the folder and work up. This time the overlap will be slightly less than half an inch.

Don't cramp these cards together. Fourteen or fifteen master and major characters and eighteen to twenty minor characters is enough to populate most novels. If you find you need more later, start a second folder.

When the portfolio is completed, it will look like figure six.

Neat, huh? You're going to love making and using this part of your Writer's Tool Kit. All that flipping up and over like some cardsharp's

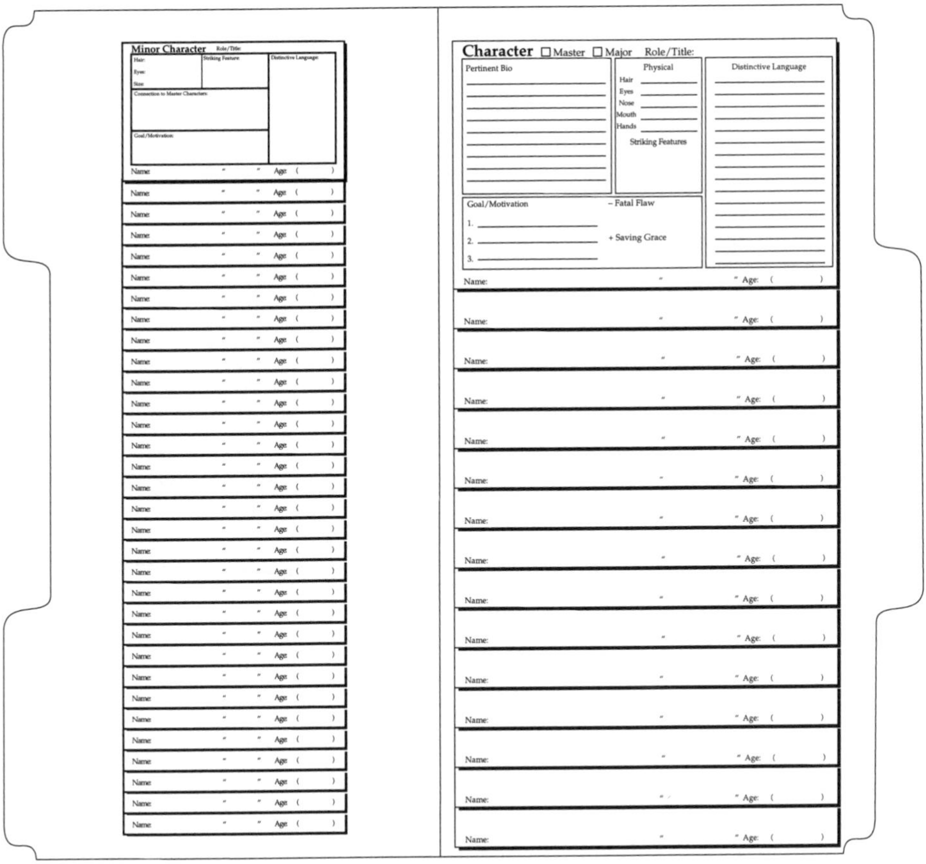

*Fig. 6. Completed character portfolio*

toy. More important, this device will save you hours of poring over loose notes and manuscript pages to find some tiny detail that's escaped you, something as simple as eye color, for example.

Two final things:

**Thing one**—You can sometimes find elaborate (expensive), hinged fingertip index files in office supply stores; and,

**Thing two**—Don't tape hinges to the back sides of your cards. They'll tend to stick up and ruin that cool tsunami wave effect.

## STEP 10: SKETCH IN YOUR SETTING

Settings are important. A good writer can transport readers anywhere in the world—and out of this world, for that matter.

And settings are a pain. Handled poorly, they can be the most boring segments of a novel, the stuff readers skip. If you've ever read one of those novels that opens with page after page of description of the physical and foreboding elements of a geographical site (are *you* admitting you're the one person in the world who reads that?), you know the problem.

## Guidelines on settings

**Treat setting as a major character.** Fill out one of the $5'' \times 8''$ cards on the right-hand side of your character portfolio. Where it says "Role/ Title," enter "Setting." On the "Name" line identify the setting. Is it a summer home on Martha's Vineyard? Yellowstone National Park? Precinct 93? An aircraft carrier at sea?

Whatever it is, go on to modify the labels and add data about the setting. When you write about the setting, give it personality, involve it in the action. If it's a barren desert, consider its saving graces. If it's a crystal palace, identify its fatal flaws (a railroad tanker full of window cleaner every month?). An inanimate setting might not have goals and motivations, but it definitely imposes rules of conduct on all characters equally, and they defy these rules at their peril. Anybody who's hiked in the mountains and slept in grizzly backcountry knows this.

**Gather pictures of your setting.** And maps and encyclopedic data. Get to know this character well. If you need more space than is available on the back of the character card, write on the back of the file folder.

**Never overdescribe your setting.** Why run the risk of boring readers? You ought to get nervous somewhere in the middle of a third consecutive sentence of description.

**Introduce a distinctive technical feature** within the scope of the overall setting. If you inject interesting, even oddball, elements into a story, you add to the intrigue. To clarify:

- In *Jaws*, we all learned about the feeding habits of sharks—license plates, for Pete's sake?
- In *Jurassic Park*, there's DNA science used to restore extinct creatures—and those mosquitoes locked in amber.

You get the picture. Just don't overdescribe it.

# 3 BUILD A FRAMEWORK FOR YOUR NOVEL'S PIECES

15 steps for building a road map that will guide you from your novel's opening to its end

Know what you are going to write before you sit down to write.

John D. MacDonald

## STEP 1: GET A GRASP OF THE BIG PICTURE

Examine this master story model in figure seven on the following page.

The master story model shows how stories are structured, from cartoons, to biblical tales, to movies, to novels, to plays.

**A quick overview of the model.** From the start of a novel to its end, a series of scenes are strung together like pearls on a necklace.

And just what is a scene?

A scene portrays action and dialogue. Characters stand in
the spotlight and move the story forward by their behavior,
words and thoughts as the author remains invisible.

A scene "takes you there to witness the action for yourself." So a scene differs from narrative devices in which the author flat out tells you what happened, as in, "Four months later, the two met again in the dank corner of the nightclub, each of them intending to kill the other." No matter how much craft an author employs, when you stand at arm's

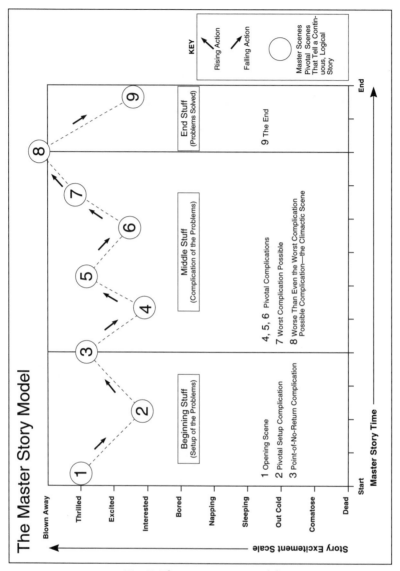

*Fig. 7. The master story model*

length from this sentence, you realize it is she talking and not one of the characters. As an author you'll be making choices about whether to portray information in an active scene or in the author shorthand of narration.

## *Master scenes*

How does a master scene differ from a scene?

> A master scene portrays your novel's most powerful action and master characters at the most critical points of the story. These critical points are always turning points characterized by complications, reversals and conflict for the master characters.

As the story model suggests, master scenes do not form a straight line. They vary, sometimes raising the level of excitement, sometimes lowering it, never falling to the level of boring. Master scenes always feature Conflict with a capital C.

What's more, master scenes fall into the three segments of a novel: beginning, middle and end, and they each fulfill a distinct purpose within that segment. The model on page 46 roughly portrays the relative space a novelist will devote to segment. In a novel of 80,000 words, a beginning might occupy 10,000 to 30,000 words. The end will use fewer than 5,000 words, and I'd recommend a lot fewer. The middle will occupy, as Paul Harvey might say, the rest of the story.

To help you get started on writing your own master scenes, I've invented a little teaching aid.

## STEP 2: CREATE YOUR OWN SCENE CARDS

Take a look at figure eight on the next page.

Now, using $5'' \times 8''$ cards, borrow as much or as little as you want from the example and make nine or ten cards for yourself. My example for a scene card no doubt devotes less room than you would like to sketch out the action. That's not a disadvantage. The more room you have, the more time you'll spend in preparatory writing, and you already know my opinion on that.

## STEP 3: SKETCH OUT THE MOST IMPORTANT SCENE IN YOUR NOVEL

Which scene is that? The master story model on page 46 identifies only master scenes.

| Scene Card ☐ Master ☐ Major ☐ Minor | Story Phase: ☐ Setup ☐ Middle ☐ End | Setting |
|---|---|---|
| Master Characters in This Scene: _____ _____ _____ _____ Other Characters in This Scene: _____ _____ _____ _____ _____ ☐ Day ☐ Night Time: _____ Must the action in this scene . . . ☐ come before or . . . ☐ after an event? What event? | Dominant Action in This Scene: Dominant Conflict: This scene is provoked by The scene's purpose is to ☐ Move the master story line ahead ☐ Introduce or develop characters ☐ Introduce or worsen a problem ☐ Solve a problem ☐ Set up later scenes ☐ Create atmosphere | Effects: ☐ Sound _____ ☐ Light _____ ☐ Smell _____ ☐ Taste _____ ☐ Touch _____ ☐ Sight _____ Dominant Effect: Segue to Next Scene: |

*Fig. 8. The scene card*

## A three-question quiz

**Question 1.** In the master story model in figure seven, which of the master scenes are the two most important scenes in a novel?

**Answer to question 1.** Master scenes one and eight, the opening scene and the climax.

**Question 2.** Of these two, which is more important?

**Question 3.** Which scene should you write first?

**Answer to questions 2 and 3.** The climax.

> **Cardinal Rule #14:** Begin your novel by writing the climactic scene first.

I admit, that's a tall order. So, if you can't write your climactic scene in detail, at least sketch it out.

Nothing wastes a writer's time like writing the opening scene of a novel without knowing where the story will go. American closet floors are replete with first chapters of novels that never got off the ground, let alone finished.

I don't always agree with Hollywood bashing, but this is one ill you can lay at the feet of Tinsel Town denizens. In the movies every character who's ever written his Great American Novel began by typing "Chapter One" and working through a stack of blank pages till the novel was done. Along the way a few pages got pulled out of the typewriter, crumpled and strewn about, but eventually the writer typed "The End," boxed his manuscript and sent it off to fame and glory.

What a lovely irony it is that scriptwriters are the very souls who perpetuate this myth. The truth is that a true genius *can* compose a novel in her head and then transcribe the tale from brain through keyboard to paper. If you consider yourself a literary wizard with a writing talent comparable to Mozart's musical brilliance, go ahead and write your novel the way they do in films. I have only one question: If you're so smart, what are you doing reading this book?

Chances are, you're somebody more like me, somebody who needs a system like the one in this book for keeping your thoughts organized so you can free up your brain to tell a passable, salable story. So stick with me, and I'll teach you how.

## Sketching out the climax

This is so simple you're going to wonder why you ever fretted about it. Begin with the top elements on the master scene card.

**Check the "Master" box.** This is a master scene.

**Write "Climax" after the words "Story Phase"** and check two boxes: "Middle" and "End." This is a bit of a formality that I use as a teaching point. Notice on the master story model that master scene eight depicts the highest excitement level in the story—literally off the chart—and that it lies on the margin between the middle of the story and the end. This

> **Cardinal Rule #15:** No scene in your novel is as important as your climax. Every scene that precedes the climax must logically build toward it, and every scene that follows the climax to the end of the story must be a logical result of it.

points out the moment in the story that sets a reader's pulse racing as you deliver the knockout punch. Here you will spend all your talent and creativity, saving nothing for your next novel. This is the destination to which every other scene is aimed, the scene that satisfies or disappoints, the part of the story that will generate either a word-of-mouth following or a death blow to your burgeoning writing career. Should you write a dynamite opening but only a firecracker climax for your first novel, you needn't bother trying to sell it.

Identify the setting or settings where the climactic action will take place. Then move to the left one-third of the scene card.

Write in the names of all your master characters. A scene this important must contain at least your three most important players.

Identify other characters that will appear in this scene, if you know them well enough.

Indicate the time and timing of your scene. Again, if you already know them. These elements pertain to scenes that must be put in order, and this segment of the card allows you to write reminders to yourself for sequencing. Now move to the center segment of the scene card, where the most important stuff goes.

Sketch in the action that will take place in this scene, using the back of the card, if necessary. Way back in chapter one, we discussed the heroic ending as one essential element of a salable novel idea. You might want to take a moment to review the ground we covered then. At a minimum you should refer to the nugget you wrote to express the concept of your own novel. In it you might well have stated or implied a climactic scene or an ending that suggests a scene to use as a climax. If you want, you can reread a sentence from the opening paragraph of chapter one: "A great white shark terrorizes a resort until three men hunt down the animal and kill it after a titanic struggle that costs one of the trio his life." The climactic scene is suggested right there in the latter half of the sentence.

Remember that idea of a titanic struggle in creating your climax. Also remember this guideline: a powerful dilemma resolved in the heroic character's favor. Clearly, if you've thought about your ending at all—even something as broad as "happily ever after"—you ought to have at least a vague idea of a scene that brings about the ending you envision.

The best way to illustrate is to use the example from *Jaws* and flesh out what is suggested for that climactic scene.

The film's heroic characters meet up with the devil shark at sea and try an escalating series of techniques to catch the great white. At first they use a fishing pole, which is downright pathetic. They shoot the fish with bullets, to no effect. Then comes a series of harpoons attached to barrels. For a while this tactic seems to work, and the men even tie the wounded creature's lines to their boat, the *Orca*. But the strategy backfires. Rather than the boat towing the shark, the fish starts pulling the craft backward, swamping it with water, threatening to sink it. Next the shark chases the boat, and the *Orca*'s captain, obsessed with killing the animal, blows the engine by overrevving it, leaving them dead in the water. The shark smashes into the hull. *Orca* takes on water. The scientist goes overboard in a shark cage and scuba gear, hoping to stick the great white with a poison dart. The shark shatters the cage, apparently killing the scientist, then flops on board, swallows the captain alive, takes another run and slithers aboard again for the sheriff. The sheriff delays his own death by tossing an air tank into the shark's mouth. The beast backs off but makes a final run. The sheriff shoots at the shark—which we've already seen has little effect on the great white. Odd, too, that the sheriff is chanting a death wish. "Come on," he says, over and over. But wait. The sheriff is not shooting at the shark but the air tank. He hits it at the last instant with his final bullet, blowing the shark to bits.

Arguably, you could say that only the last encounter with the sheriff is the truly climactic scene. If you like putting the action onto several cards instead of one, fine. What's important is to get the essentials down in proper order. And here's a tip:

> **Tip:** When sketching your action on scene cards, use snippets of dialogue and the artful phrases that you'll want to write into your novel—write them onto the card so you'll have them later when setting down your first draft.

Oh, and another thing, remember that audiocassette recorder I suggested in your list of supplies?

> **Tip:** Keep your tape recorder handy when sketching out your novel. Use it to record notes to yourself for plot twists and ideas to transfer to scene cards later in the process.

I'll discuss further requirements of your climax in a moment. For now, let's complete the other segments of this card.

**Note the principal conflict portrayed in the scene** or the major obstacle to be overcome. In *Jaws*, the conflict is the ultimate life-and-death clash between men and beast.

**Indicate what brought the scene about** by telling what causes the conflict.

**Check whatever purposes the scene fulfills.** Your climactic scene solves the predominant conflict inherent in your novel and sets up the ending. Every scene in your novel must accomplish one of the following:

## Purposes of a scene
- Move the novel's story line forward.
- Introduce or develop characters.
- Introduce or worsen a problem.
- Solve a problem.
- Set up later scenes.
- Create atmosphere.

Pay attention to the following cardinal rule and you'll save yourself a lot of time in the writing of your novel.

---

**Cardinal Rule #16:** When contemplating a scene, if you can't clearly establish the purpose for a scene, *don't create that scene.* Use narration to make your point and convey your readership to the next scene.

---

Now move to the right-hand side of the card.

**Check off the sensory effects** you'll want to highlight in your climactic scene. You might check all the boxes for a scene as important as this one. Lesser scenes might feature only one effect. For instance: Remember in *Jaws* when the scientist cut open a shark and produced an auto license plate? The sensory effects included the sight of blood, the feel of the sharkskin and, of course, the stench.

**Identify the major sensory effect** you intend to use to cap off the scene. You won't want to give equal weight to every sensory impression you create. Use this space to remind yourself of the primary feeling you'll want to leave with your readers. In the climactic scene of the film *Jaws*, I'd say it was the sight and sound of the explosion, a kind of combined special effect. I'd also say it was enhanced by the sound track, that "shark-alert" music that reached its crescendo the instant before the explosion.

**Write a segue you might use to transition to the next scene.** Don't ignore this little item. The best novelists use well-crafted transitions to transport readers from one sentence to the next, one paragraph to the next, one scene to the next and one chapter to the next. A *segue* (pronounced SEG-way) can be a word of dialogue or narration, an image or a piece of continued action that compels a reader to stay with you from one segment of your novel to the next, no matter how hungry or tired she may be. A segue often creates a mirror image of an earlier phrase or even a flashback to previous action.

Continuing with our climactic scene in *Jaws*, here's the visual segue: The sheriff (and audience) is both drained and relieved at the apparent death of the shark following the explosion of the air tank. Yet a sudden fountain of bubbles and turbulent water beside him can only mean one thing: It's back. Throughout the movie, the roiling of water is a prelude to shark attack. This time, though, the disturbance yields another, happier result: The scientist, whom we thought dead, surfaces from the seabed where he's been hiding. The segue takes us to the movie's end scene, the pair of them swimming off toward shore into the sunset, happily ever after—or at least till *Jaws II* and *III*.

Finished with your climactic scene card? Congratulations, you have taken the concept embodied in your nugget and moved it well forward in the process of writing your novel.

Now you have just one more task to perform before moving on to sketch out the next most important scene of your novel. Take another run at your climax, scrubbing it with the following checklist.

## *Ten elements of a climactic scene*

√ **A titanic, epic and final struggle.** This applies as much to a romance as to an action tale. Your most powerful scene of conflict, whether emotional or visual, takes place at the climax. You must thrill your readers—no, you must blow them away—with all the dazzling literary brilliance you can muster.

What's more, no major action should be scheduled to follow the climax. Otherwise, that action will be—what else?—*anticlimactic.*

√ **Heroic character confronts her worthy adversary.** Minor characters and even most major characters do not count for much in a climactic scene. That's one reason why so many novelists have trouble setting up a climax. Often the author forces the heroine either to take an incredible (in the sense of *not* credible) risk or to pull a boneheaded stunt to isolate protagonist against antagonist. How many times have you known the hero to neglect calling the police (or the police officer neglect to call backup) and dash into a darkened warehouse to confront an army of villains?

√ **Heroic conflict resolved in the heroic character's favor.** Do not slay the heroic character. Even if the heroine's victory is bittersweet, it must be a victory, usually of good over evil. Even if she does not win the heart of her romantic interest, she will have proven herself deserving of it.

√ **An important lesson for your heroic character.** That the heroic character learns something valuable from her struggle is one important outcome of the climactic scene of conflict. No need to be preachy about it, but face it—it's almost a tenet of human experience that the most dramatic events of our lives teach us something of value. Our scars cost us something, perhaps innocence or purity, but we also wear them as badges of learning.

√ **Avoidance of coincidence, cavalry or divine intervention.** Put another way, your heroic characters decide the novel's crucial battle. A lucky coincidence might save a character from ruin once in your novel. If it happens in an early scene, you won't offend. Try it again at the climax, and your book, in the unlikely event an editor lets the coincidence stand, will be thrown around many a living room in disgust. Quick now, what's one of the most popular movies of recent time that features the intervention of cavalry at the last instant to save the heroic characters? And odd cavalry at that. Did you choose *Jurassic Park*? Did it bother you as much as it did me that T-rex saved the day from the velociraptors before the heroic characters could determine their own fate? Totally bogus. Don't try it yourself until you achieve the status of Michael Crichton.

**No new material introduced into the climax.** No new characters, no special remedies, no surprise intrusions of fact. It's perfectly fair to lay out seemingly innocuous facts and circumstances early in a novel, elements that only come into play in the climax—that air tank in *Jaws*, for example. Early on the sheriff mishandles a tank while loading the *Orca* for the shark pursuit. The scientist and captain reprimand him, and not much is made of air tanks again until the sheriff fires a bullet into the tank lodged in the great white's jaws. Incidentally, this technique is often called *foreshadowing*—planting a fact or demonstrating a behavior that seems insignificant until later when it becomes pivotal.

**Avoidance of flashbacks.** Once you've set the climactic scene in motion, don't look back. If you've set things up properly, you won't need to stop the forward momentum and review some past activity. Keep the story moving by action and dialogue.

**Lack of explanation.** Explanation—*exposition* is the technical term—drags any scene down, but using it in the climax will kill your story. I direct your attention to *Jurassic Park* again. Remember the video orientation about DNA within the movie when the scientists first arrived at the park? Although cleverly done, with wit and visuals, the movie grinds to a halt so the audience can hear the explanation of how modern dinosaurs could exist. One word describes that scene: boring. Imagine if that had been done at the climax. *Fatally* boring.

Also avoid the technique of the parlor mystery in which everybody sits around while the heroic character deduces aloud and at length and finally points out the murderer to the gasps of other characters and the yawns of readers. Resolve your major conflict by action, including meaningful dialogue, if you will, but not by the artificial device of the author putting explanatory words into a character's mouth.

√ **A logical conclusion.** Throughout your novel one character's motives coincide or clash with another's, creating dramatic tension and driving the story in a logical direction. If you can set it up that a character would rationally experience a change of heart or mind that skews the direction of the novel, no problem. But how persuasive is it when a ruthless killer terrorist, who's arbitrarily been gunning down everybody who frowns his way, suddenly and illogically engages the heroine in conversational patter, giving her the opportunity to make good her inevitable escape? In today's movies this happens all too often.

In the television *Batman* series, the device of lowering the dynamic duo into a tank of _____ (boiling oil, crocodiles, piranhas, acid—you fill in the blank) and leaving the room so Batman could retrieve some self-rescue gadget out of his Batbelt was standard, campy, delightful fare. But that doesn't make it believable.

In his latest novel, one best-selling novelist invented a character that had been so thoroughly motivated by the love of her father, country and not-so-heroic hero that she acted in some of the dumbest ways and suddenly and illogically gave up all to steal the hero's cash and vanish. You can't explain such a trick except to call it the last-ditch device of an author gone lazy from success. What made this instance most despicable was the author letting the readers in on the woman's thoughts earlier in the novel. As we followed along on her mental process, she never once suggested she was capable of anything but the purest motives and most devoted behavior. So when she turned into a cheat of the first kind against all logic in the closing pages of the story, the novel turned into a cheat of the worst kind.

*No tricks.*

√ **A sense of wonder.** Even if you aren't blessed with a rich imagination, you can still write a salable novel just by not boring readers. You can write a memorable novel by filling readers with a sense of wow in your master scenes, especially the climax. Spring your most inventive surprises here. Contrary to the conventional wisdom about impressions, your novel will be judged by its final impression not its first.

---

**Cardinal Rule #17:** What matters is not so much what people say when they pick up your novel as what they say after they put it down.

---

It's worth repeating: Spend your best creativity in this scene, saving nothing for your next novel.

## STEP 4: CREATE YOUR NOVEL'S OPENING SCENE

Take out another scene card. Time to carve out a beginning. *Finally.* The place you've been so eager to be.

Fill in blanks just as you did with the climactic scene. Opening scenes set up the rest of the novel. The job of an opening is to grab a reader. What elements should you include in your novel's opening so your books will fly off the shelves of bookstores? Here's a laundry list of things to consider and check off for inclusion in your own novel.

### *Stuff to open with*

√ **A great first line.** I talked about this before. If you haven't already done so, write one now, and include its essence on your scene card. Kaye Gibbons is a modern master of riveting first lines. She opens *Ellen Foster* with: "When I was little I would think of ways to kill my daddy." Once this narrator grasps you with that sentence, she just doesn't let go. How are you not going to read the rest of that book?

√ **A high level of excitement**—high action, high drama, high emotion, the works. As you can see on the master story model, your opening should contain, or at least suggest, a level of intensity just below that of the climax.

✓ **A likable heroic character** with a worthy goal.

✓ **A formidable adversary.** If she isn't introduced in this scene, she ought to be suggested at least.

✓ **Serious obstacles for the heroic character** to overcome before she can achieve her worthy goal. This is true even in low comedy. Remember the film *Dumb and Dumber*? OK, dumb example.

✓ **A writing style that's easy on the eyes**—conversational, natural, lyrical, literate and striking, yet unadorned.

✓ **Action.** Not necessarily car chases and explosions. I mean movement, dialogue and a sense of things happening rather than lengthy descriptions and internal musings by your characters.

✓ **A clear image of an interesting setting.**

✓ **A feeling of danger or suspense.**

✓ **A touch of humor or at least irony.**

✓ **A proper balance between the two.** This item refers to an apparent contradiction between the preceding two elements. It means that you set the predominant tone of your story in the opening. Is it high drama or low comedy? This tone should remain consistent, but you ought to leaven a predominant tone of humor with a touch of seriousness and vice versa. This is a technique of pacing, which I discuss in detail later.

✓ **A foreshadowing** of important things to come. In a movie, a kind of preopening scene often takes place while the credits run. Remember the nighttime skinny-dipper who disappeared underwater in *Jaws*? And the laborer who was pulled into the raptor cage in *Jurassic Park*? Fiction writers often use the technique, too, and the scenes are packaged as prologues. In such a prologue, the villain is often introduced in the commission of his villainy to elevate tension in the book's opening, to grab readers (dragging them underwater and into cages) and to foreshadow what might happen to any character in the book if he's not careful. If you write such a preopener, don't call it a prologue because readers so often skip them. If you plan to use a preopener, call it chapter one, and if it doesn't introduce your heroic character, keep it brief—no more than six pages.

Sketch in the elements of your preopener on a separate card.

## STEP 5: LAY OUT YOUR MASTER SCENE CARDS

You're ready to connect the dots. Don't laugh that it may only be two dots. Just do it. Clear off a tabletop. In the upper left of your space, lay down the one or two cards you used to capture your opening. Place your climactic scene card in the upper-right area of the space. Time to fill in the blank between the two.

Start by positioning your nugget, that 40-word draft of your novel that contains the overall context of the action. Put it somewhere in the center and above all else. Tape it to the wall where you never lose sight of it. From here on out, you craft scenes that carry your story—and readers—on a logical journey of fiction from your beginning to your end. Later, when your required scenes are cemented into place, you'll be deciding how to create devices for taking readers from one scene to the next. For now you simply perform a two-step operation for relating the story.

### TELLING YOUR NOVEL'S STORY

**One—Review your previous card.** In this case, the card or cards from your opening, to refresh your memory about what action takes place there.

**Two—Tell what happens next.** Simple as that. Over the course of a novel, you'll ask yourself a thousand times: What happens next?

## STEP 6: WRITE YOUR CENTRAL STORY IN "HEADLINES" ON 3″×5″ CARDS

Use only headlines to tell your central story the first time through. The cards will force you into using telegraphic language and limit you to nouns and verbs—a good practice to follow when you begin composing your prose.

I'll illustrate from a novel I'm now marketing, *Cottage 13*. Each of the following bullet items goes on a separate 3″ × 5″ card.

## Scene headlines for Cottage 13

After sketching in a preopening scene showing a delinquent, Earl, stalking his junior high teacher, I asked myself:

> **What happens next?**

- Lamar enters Cottage 13, the juvenile lockup. First time. Stench of prison.
  > **What happens next?**
- L. meets custody sergeant Byrnes. Highlight difference in size.
  > **What happens next?**
- Sergeant Byrnes gives L. nickel tour of jail.
  > **What happens next?**
- L. meets the vicious Earl. Instant hatred between the two. Lamar envisions smashing Earl's face. First sign of rage.
  > **What happens next?**
- L. visits barren classroom.
  > **What happens next?**
- L. flashes back to job interview with warden.
  > **What happens next?**
- L. goes home. (Fresh air outside.) Reveal fiancée has left him.
  > **What happens next?**
- L. showers to rid self of jail stench. Flashes back to brutal childhood.

And so on, until you have a stack of cards that tells your central story from beginning to climax to end. If you have gaps between certain points in the story, don't fret. If you get stumped, don't worry. If you're worried about pacing, subplots, characterization, motivation, dialogue and the rest, don't. Just relax. I have a few tips to help you keep the lid on anxiety during this little exercise.

## Tips for writing scene headlines

**Stick to the main story line.** Just write the headlines for what happens between your master characters as they go about contending in the central conflict in your novel. If an unrelated scene or subplot or plot twist asserts itself out of nowhere, set it down on a card, put it aside and return to the main story line.

**Be brief about it.** Get as much of the story down as quickly as possible in story sequence. Work fast. You can come back later to enlarge upon your headlines.

**Keep moving.** If you find yourself stymied, move forward to the next point where you can pick up the story. Fill in gaps later.

**Keep it informal.** For now, forget about grammar and choosing the perfect word from a thesaurus. Remember to spill your tale as if you were telling a friend about a movie you've just seen: "The T-rex breaks through the fence, and the goofy lawyer tries to hide in the restroom. The T-rex makes a meal of him—right off the toilet." I'd put the elements of that scene on a card using those very words.

**Capture your gems of genius.** If a witty dialogue exchange springs to mind, write it out. Copy your insightful phrase to a card so you don't lose it. Write reminders to yourself, as I did in the *Cottage 13* example with "Reveal fiancée has left him."

**Spend time in multiple sessions** capturing your main story line. Sometimes your creativity burns out from overuse. Put this exercise aside, and come back to it later. A fresh mind gives rise to fresh ideas.

**Be ready for flashes of brilliance** that occur to you when you least expect them. Carry a stack of blank cards with you. Keep the audiocassette recorder handy. From here to the finish of your novel, like a Boy Scout, be prepared. Capture ideas that burst from your subconscious. Put down random thoughts that might later go into your novel even if you aren't able to position them right now.

**Capitalize on nuggets of discovery and mystery.** You entertain readers best when you engage them in your novel. In the *Cottage 13* examples, I'd underline the item about revealing that Lamar's fiancée has left him. In the actual writing of the scene, I'd let it be known she was gone without telling why. The reader wonders: What happened there? Was it the guy's rage? (Yes, incidentally. As revealed in that scene where he envisions smashing Earl's face.) Later the reader will learn that she was right about the reason and congratulate herself for anticipating the writer's intention.

**Highlight tiebacks.** If I've given you the impression that writing a novel should be a process of telling only (this happened, then this, then this. . . .), I apologize right here. The author doesn't write in a straight, plodding line. He often refers to previous issues. He does this to update story elements, to round them out, to peel back layers of mystery, allowing characters to discover what readers already know and to maintain a story's continuity.

A plan for such a tieback occurs in the bullet cards listed for *Cottage 13*. When Lamar enters the juvenile lockup, he's hit in the face by the stench of jail. Later, as he goes home, he is struck by the freshness of the outside air—something he might not otherwise notice. At home, he feels a need to shower, to wash away the smell of jail. Peter Rubie, author of *The Elements of Storytelling* (Wiley Books for Writers), calls this technique *circular writing* and tells how to enrich the texture of your story using it. I love his discussion of circular writing, although I can't quite get used to the term itself. I suppose it reminds me too much of the energy I sometimes spend marching in circles as if my left shoe were nailed to the floor.

**Don't economize on cards.** They're cheap, and this is a crucial exercise, so don't try to save money by cramming multiple scenes onto a single index card. If you need to reposition a scene later to another part of the story, you won't have to create a new card to split the action.

**Lay out your 3″ × 5″ cards in story sequence.** After you've captured the essence of your story on cards, you're ready for positioning them. Here you decide on the order for telling your main story line. Under the master scene cards for the opening, place your 3″ × 5″ cards in columns to show the sequence you'll be using. If the action uses several smaller scenes, keep those cards in their own columns.

When you're finished laying out this main story line, don't be surprised if you've created enough cards to outgrow your tabletop. Don't be surprised if you find you have to relocate story cards to the carpet and fill up the floor space of an entire room.

**Conduct some preliminary research.** Don't get hung up on research in the early stages of laying out your novel. Just skim the literature within the arena of your writing so you don't blunder irreparably. You wouldn't want to base the premise of your story on December snows in Australia only to find out later that December is midsummer Down Under.

Track down the best sources on your topic and setting, and look them over to prevent such a disaster. If new ideas for scenes crop up, write them on cards and insert them into your story sequence.

## STEP 7: IDENTIFY YOUR PIVOTAL COMPLICATION SCENES

Stand back and survey your card layout. Anytime you've sorted cards into separate columns, you've probably indicated a change in your novel's direction. This is one way to identify a turning point in the story, or, as I call it, a pivotal complication scene (PCS). Such a scene is important enough to deserve its own cardinal rule.

> **Cardinal Rule #18:** Anytime in the course of a novel that the story changes direction because of problems introduced or complications resolved between master characters, write it as a master scene.

And, to identify it as a possible PCS, place a red check or some other identifying mark on the $3'' \times 5''$ card.

To illustrate what a PCS looks like, recall the movie *Jurassic Park*. Soon after the high-tension preopener of the worker being dragged into a raptor cage, the film cuts to the badlands of Montana. Here we meet two of the film's many heroic characters, Alan and Ellie. Alan gives us the explanation of how raptors hunt in packs, foreshadowing later deaths in the climactic scene. And we get a glimpse of the friendship between the two scientists, their dedication to their work of paleontology and Alan's dislike of kids. Interesting stuff, but after the fright of the preopener, there's no way to describe this scene except as falling action, not exactly boring, but certainly not blood-chilling, either.

Cue the helicopter. Enter the park's creator, John Hammond, to introduce one heck of a complication to the scientists' lives. He offers research money to entice them on a weekend consulting trip, and, after some haggling, they accept. This is the first pivotal complication in the film's opening, one that sets up action for the remainder of the story, identified in the master story model with the numeral 2.

Another example, this time from the sample headline cards from *Cottage 13*. Review my collection of opening headlines. Which do you imagine is the first pivotal scene and the one that would be written as a master scene?

I included three pivotal master scenes in that list. I began with the first confrontation with Earl. The conflict between two adversaries, the revelation of Lamar's capacity for rage, the foreshadowing of a showdown between them—all these elements elevate the importance of this scene.

By the way, the second master scene is the flashback to the job interview with the warden, which features dramatic conflict between the two and suggests that Lamar has a history of trouble in public schools. Third is the flashback to an instance of abuse suffered at the hands of his father. You might have chosen other headlines to designate as pivotal complications and thus write as master scenes. If this were your novel, you might write the first scene with Lamar as a master scene because you're introducing the heroic character. Fine. Your choice is every bit as valid as mine—as long as you're able to establish in structuring the scene that it will be pivotal.

## Essential elements of a pivotal complication

Use a pivotal complication to present a problem that changes the direction of your novel and sets up action to come. When you sketch out a situation that either promises to, or does, throw characters into conflict (we just *know* the scientists are going to become dinosaur bait when they agree to travel to Jurassic Park. And, after their first meeting, how can Lamar and Earl *not* face off later in the classroom?), plan to write it as a pivotal complication scene.

Always involve master characters in a pivotal complication.

A pivotal complication must be written as a scene, with master characters determining the change in direction or introduction of a problem and not the author slapping down a problem in narrative form. In *Cottage 13* Lamar throws Earl against the wall and draws back a fist to hit him—before Lamar snaps out of it and realizes it's a daydream. This technique is superior to the author telling you: "Lamar felt like hitting Earl in the face."

Remember that a pivotal complication *often* results from action that precedes it, maintaining your story's logic.

Never forget that besides thickening the plot, a pivotal complication *always* points logically to your climactic scene, even if you artfully conceal that connection from your readers for now. Later, when the reader reflects in wonder at your creativity, she will discover the connection.

Take time to identify such scenes among the beginning scenes of your novel. If you haven't yet identified where the middle begins, don't worry.

Just continue identifying pivotal scenes until you feel certain you've found your way out of the beginning.

## STEP 8: TRANSFER PIVOTAL COMPLICATIONS TO MASTER SCENE CARDS

You already know how to fill out a master scene card. Complete one for each of the PCSs you've already identified. Be thorough about this step. If you find yourself being diverted to create batches of headlines on $3'' \times 5''$ cards, good. Your mission is to enlarge and enrich your story from here on out.

## STEP 9: FIND AND CRAFT YOUR POINT-OF-NO-RETURN COMPLICATION

This is the complication that bridges the setup and middle of your novel. This scene ought to be self-evident by now. You've worked with dozens of cards sketching the sequence of your novel. Sooner or later one scene lends itself to being labeled the point of no return.

An example will clarify my logic for you. In *Jurassic Park* we marveled through all those scenes that revealed the wondrous existence of dinosaurs, including the ominous and all-too-intelligent raptors. We saw the park's safeguards, computers and staff. We met John Hammond's grandchildren, that rascally Dennis Nedry (Newman!) and the just-this-side-of-sleazy mathematician, Ian Malcolm. We learned of an imminent tropical storm and saw many glitches in the so-called fail-safe park operation. Oh, yes, and we fidgeted through that video DNA orientation designed to set up in considerable detail the techno-justification for the park's (and the story's) existence.

All of these scenes comprised the story's setup or beginning, introducing characters, situations and problems (not to mention any number of disguised solutions that were to come into play later—remember how the computer wizardry of Hammond's granddaughter, Lex, proved to be pivotal in the climax?).

As to the point-of-no-return complication (PoNRC) in *Jurassic Park*: From the moment the computer-controlled auto tour went dead right outside the T-rex enclosure, nothing in the rest of the film was going to be undone. None of the characters could back out of the film. As we used to say in the Army, the situation had gone to the point of OBE, overcome by events. That was the PoNRC.

So tight was the setup in this film that, literally, nobody but Superman himself could have fled this movie unscathed from this moment onward. The tropical storm cut off escape by helicopter or ship. Nedry's sabotage of all computer safeguards had unlocked all gates and doors and shut off power to the electric fences, and his subsequent death prevented the undoing of his mischief.

Beyond all doubt, the characters in this story had been thrown to the (prehistoric) wolves. The story from here on would play out in the form of one complication after another, beginning with the escape of T-rex, the situation continually worsening for the good guys. They knew it, and you knew it.

That's a PoNRC for all time and one of the reasons the stories of Michael Crichton and Steven Spielberg are so popular.

Since this example illustrates so well, let's draw some lessons for writing your own PoNRC.

## Essentials of a point-of-no-return complication

**A thorough setup followed by things falling into place.** In this critical complication the bulk of your exquisite preparatory details click, creating a sense of wonder. Because the set pieces have been cemented into position so convincingly, this powerful scene is at once believable and inevitable.

**Strong, believable motivations and actions** of the film's characters. Coincidence alone will not suffice to bring about a scene this important. Granted, several coincidences do come into play all at once in *Jurassic Park*: the arrival of the storm, the timing of Nedry's theft, the positioning of the automated tour when the systems fail. As I've already said, a bit of coincidence in the early part of a story isn't so bad. What rescues the scene is the sense that all the characters in the story, including dinos, have been positioned by their own competing or cooperative motivations or by the actions of other characters. Once that's established, a coincidence or two—even one so influential as a huge storm—seems barely a factor.

**A strong sense of suspense.** Your characters, even if they're playing in a romantic comedy, must feel trapped in the PoNRC. What's more, your readers should feel the same quickening of pulse and shortness of breath the characters are feeling in anticipation of what is to come. Remember the seismic effect of T-rex footfalls in causing ripples in water? That image has become an instant suspense classic.

**A crucial decision point.** Because of the situation that unfolds in your PoNRC scene, the heroic characters must make choices that affect the novel all the way through to the climactic scene and its logical ending. Often a heroic character will make a wrong choice because he thinks it will solve all the problems he's created so far in your story; instead he finds out he's created a new set of quandaries.

Final words on your point-of-no-return complication: Don't worry about it. You may even disguise a heroic character's fateful decision by downplaying it. Later your readers will enjoy a wondrous moment of discovery when the importance of that decision dawns. So if your PoNRC doesn't hit you between the eyes right now, just move on to the next step. Sooner or later, it will make its appearance.

## STEP 10: IDENTIFY PIVOTAL COMPLICATION SCENES IN THE MIDDLE OF YOUR NOVEL AND TRANSFER THEM TO MASTER SCENE CARDS

Same drill as before. Sift your stacks of cards, isolate pivotal scenes and transfer them in greater detail onto master scene cards.

### Essential considerations for a novel's middle

**Escalating complications.** The heroic character confronts one situation after another. Each set of new problems she faces raises the ante in her high-stakes game. If she overcomes one set of problems, any relief she feels (and readers feel) is transient at best. Adversarial forces go to work to create a worse, more complicated set of problems. The rising action in each pivotal scene reaches a new, higher peak each time the scene plays out.

**Characters' decisions rule.** Each complication in the middle of your novel is decided by the choices the characters make, choices that often lead to a worsening of the problem. Beware: An author who resorts to coincidence to resolve a pivotal complication in the middle of his novel risks ruining his story.

**As before, all complications point toward the climactic scene.**

**The heroic character faces an impossible complication.** She must draw upon every ounce of her (and her author's) creativity, skill and strength to escape this situation.

A worse than impossible complication leads to the climactic scene. This is the stuff of which the great stories are made: Worse than impossible complications resolved artfully leave readers exhausted at the outcome and marveling in awe at the author's ability to deliver a compelling package. Since you've already spent some time shaping your climactic scene, let's move on.

## STEP 11: SKETCH OUT YOUR ENDING

Your ending ought to write itself. In simplest terms, an ending is an aftermath of the climactic scene as the writing trails off to the words "The End." You'll not be introducing any more complications. You ought not belabor any of the lessons you taught. Tie up the loose ends of subplots, clean up any remaining details, shut out the lights and close the last page behind you. Here's a brief list of elements for you to consider in shaping an ending.

### *Considerations for endings*

**Be brief.** This above all. If you have any brilliance left over, you've erred. Don't tack it onto the end. Instead, go back and create new scenes or narration, planting your gems earlier in the story.

**Be definitive in your resolution.** Be mysterious and suspenseful anywhere else in your novel, but you must resolve all the doubtful issues by the time the climactic scene rolls around. If you have issues that cannot be resolved by humanity, then you owe your heroic character the insight to recognize this, thus letting him off the hook. Consider it a misdemeanor to be coy with readers anywhere in a novel, but a felony to do so in the ending.

**Resist the urge to preach.** Enough said.

So much for master scenes.

## STEP 12: IDENTIFY AND ADD DETAIL TO
## YOUR MAJOR SCENES

When I say, "Go," transfer some more headlines from your remaining $3'' \times 5''$ cards onto the $5'' \times 8''$ scene cards, checking "Major" and filling in the remaining blanks and checking the proper boxes.

I haven't said, "Go," because I don't want you to kill yourself in this exercise. Take a few minutes to absorb the following.

## Guidelines to major scenes

Recognize that major scenes are not pivotal, that is, they advance a story but they do not change the direction of the story as master scenes do. Consequently, you should expend the bulk of your effort, both quantitatively and qualitatively, on master scenes. Major scenes, minor scenes and narrative devices will fill the spaces between those master scenes. A major scene involves major characters and possibly even master characters. Although not pivotal, a major scene's function will be one of the following: to move the master story line ahead, to develop characters, to worsen a problem or to set up later scenes. For instance, recall the scene in *Jurassic Park* where that scoundrel Nedry gets lost on the way to the ship dock and falls into the jaws of the hooded dinosaur. To me, that's a major scene. If its purpose were only to show a villain getting his comeuppance, I'd downgrade it to a minor scene, but since Nedry held the secret to turning on the park's computers, his death worsens the complications for everybody else in the story.

Don't expend effort writing major scenes—for now. Other than copying and adding detail to a scene you've envisioned at this stage, don't dive into your major scenes until you've dealt with all your master scenes.

In the next chapter you'll write the first draft of your novel as first drafts of all your master scenes. Why write a couple thousand words of a major scene, bringing to life the exquisite misery of trekking across the desert on a burro, only to see them fizzle later and be reduced to a couple lines of narrative? As in: "After two days of dragging the bony burro across the Mojave, the trekkers' can-do spirit evaporated. They strangled the burro and ate the best parts of it, though there were no best parts, and the friends' peppy relationship mutated into a seething attitude of 'Shrivel up and die, you gravy-sucking pig.' "

Use major scenes to pace your novel. *Pacing*. Talk about a term that gets thrown about in manuals about writing. Fact is, I've thrown it about myself in earlier pages. So far, all I've done is suggest you can increase the pace of your novel by elevating the tension of complications, especially in the scenes of rising action that precede and include the climactic scene. Problem is, I haven't told you how. That's the trouble with all writing manuals. They tell you plenty of *what* but far too little *how*. So, what's pacing?

Pacing comes in two forms: the grand-scale pacing in the overall scheme of the novel and the small-scale pacing that takes place within scenes, paragraphs and sentences.

Small-scale pacing is central to the craft of writing, so we'll deal with that in the next two chapters. But you must employ grand-scale pacing now as you plan your novel, organizing it into scenes of varying importance. Every decision on how to sequence a scene is a pacing decision. This leads us to a rule telling you how to pace a novel:

---

**Cardinal Rule #19:** You elevate the grand-scale pace of your novel by bunching master scenes; likewise, you relax that pace by inserting major scenes, minor scenes and various narrative devices between your master scenes.

---

If you think about it, this is obvious. Even Dean Koontz, the celebrated master of sustaining high tension for page after page in his thrillers, can't write every scene off the chart of our master story model. Somewhere in there he has to allow himself, his characters and his readers a breather. Believe it or not, even the highest of highs eventually becomes mundane to the normals among us. Can you imagine riding even the most thrilling roller coaster hour after hour for a day? The very concept of roller coaster implies downs as well as ups. If the thing kept going up and up, never dropping, it'd be downright boring. In St. William Elementary School, the nuns tried to drill the idea of heaven into me. The hereafter came off as a joint full of numbing holiness and no place for kids like me. I had to ask, "Sister, can you have a BB gun in heaven?" She gave it a moment's thought and said with some caution, "I suppose." Wow! Maybe heaven wouldn't be so bad after all. "But can you shoot birds with it?" It was an idea I should have left unspoken, one that earned me a whack on the head and made me stop striving for heaven.

Variety is the name of the game in setting the grand-scale pace of your novel. If I were to represent this visually, this is what it would look like on a revised Master Story Model (see figure nine).

Notice two ways in which master scenes increase pace. The intensity within scenes rises *and* the number of scenes bunch up at critical points, particularly at the point-of-no-return complication and the climactic

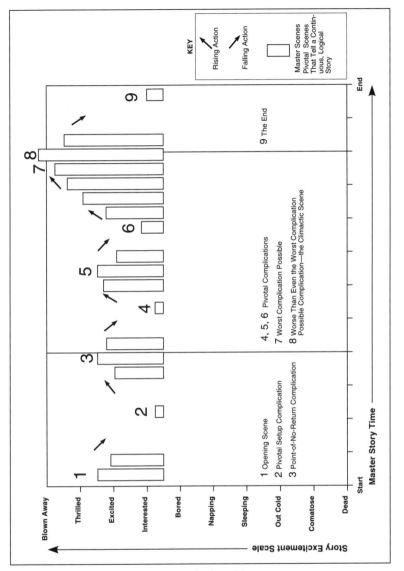

*Fig. 9. Increasing pace by bunching master scenes*

scene. Spaces between master scenes are filled with major scenes, minor scenes and narrative.

Remember the example headlines I gave you from *Cottage 13*? The ones I identified as master scenes? After I'd sketched those out, the following became major scenes:

- L. meets custody sergeant Byrnes. Highlight difference in size.
- L. goes home. (Fresh air outside.) Reveal fiancée has left him.

I treated the following as a minor scene:

- L. visits barren classroom.

It allowed me to disengage Lamar from his new enemy and show what his workplace looked like.

Identify and add detail to the major scenes you know you'll use as pacing devices between master scenes in your novel. If in doubt about a scene, don't labor over it. Go on to the next $3'' \times 5''$ card.

**Ignore minor scenes and narrative devices for now.** Novels change in unexpected ways, even for the people writing them. Inevitably you'll downgrade some of your master scenes as the novel begins to take shape. And many a minor scene will develop into a full-blown master scene as a minor character or plot twist asserts itself. I recognize that, no matter how systematic you treat this business of writing, it's like a battle. Once the first shot is fired, events take their own course. Detailed battle plans fly out the window.

So, don't write minor scenes until the writing of your master scenes is complete.

## STEP 13—IDENTIFY OBVIOUS SUBPLOTS

Don't get too wrapped up in subplots, either. If you know what they are, fine. You may have used any number of cards detailing a string of scenes that deals with a subplot issue.

For instance, you might envision the heroine's husband carrying on an extramarital affair. You know that the husband will be seen interacting with his lover. You plan to show how the affair is initiated, how it progresses and why it becomes a pivotal event in the wife's life. If you find you can't combine all those scenes into sequence because the action in the subplot is spaced over the course of the novel, no problem. Just keep each subplot stack separate from the main story line for now. Position those cards later, after writing the main story line. For now, all you need to remember is this:

---

Cardinal Rule #20: A subplot *must* establish a direct connection to the main story line, advancing and complicating the story. If a subplot is a parallel issue that never affects the outcome of the main story line in a *significant* way, leave it out.

---

Ignore this rule at your peril. If you have to sweat bullets to work one of your darling subplots into the main story, that issue is best left to your next novel. It will only detract from your current novel and confuse your readers. A quick example from *Jaws*: Did you know that in the novel the sheriff's wife carried on an extramarital affair with the scientist? I remember thinking, *What's the point?* Other than introducing a formulaic complication and obligatory sex, I still don't know. In telling the film version of the story, the affair subplot didn't appear, and nobody raised an outcry about its absence, either.

## STEP 14: TAKE STOCK

A quick review. So far, you've built a solid foundation for writing your novel. Your list of achievements include:

**A tightly written nugget statement** that crystallizes your realistic, salable idea, keeping you focused on all the other tasks you must complete in the writing of your novel.

**A cast of believable, motivated characters.** You identified your heroic characters and a few major characters by name. You gave them histories, goals and motivations. And you positioned them to play out the action of your story.

**A central story line** that conforms to the master story model, fleshing out your novel in a series of master scenes that follows a logical progression of rising action from a grabber opening to a compelling climax.

**Major scenes** sketched out in enough detail to help establish the grand pace of your novel.

**Relevant subplots,** supporting story lines that are well connected to the central story line.

**An ending** that is the logical, inevitable result of all that precedes it, most particularly your climactic scene.

## STEP 15: CONGRATULATE YOURSELF

Without ever using the dreaded word *outline*, you have created one for your novel, a workable, flexible, nonacademic model. The foundation is laid for you to write your novel without ever losing focus on where to begin. More important, you know where it should end.

Let's get to writing, shall we?

# 4 WRITE YOUR NOVEL — PUTTING THE PIECES TOGETHER

**10 steps for writing your novel intelligently, that is, without wasting time, words, effort or sanity**

> A blank page is God's way of showing you how hard it is to be God.
>
> Unknown

Everybody wants a guarantee of success. And, if it's not too much to ask, the job ought to be easy as well: Just program a few key facts into an intelligent computer, press "Enter" and watch your printer spew a page-turner.

Sorry. I can't guarantee to tell you how to write a best-seller. I *can* introduce you to a set of innovative techniques you've never seen in a writing handbook before. I *can* simplify the craft of revision. I *can* help you make sense of the overwhelming task of stringing together 80,000 or so words to tell a logical, compelling, salable story. But ease of effort? Nah. *That* I cannot guarantee. You're going to have to put some work into it.

Including revisions, there's no way around typing more than half a million keystrokes. Writing a novel is a daunting task. But if you've labored through the first three chapters of this book, creating a sound basis for writing your novel by thorough plotting and scene preparation, at least—as promised in the chapter subtitle—you won't be wasting time, words, effort or sanity.

## STEP 1: SELECT YOUR FAVORITE MASTER
## SCENE TO WRITE FIRST

Writing a novel is like eating a whale—you do it a bite at a time. So why not begin with the best parts? Don't write your first scene first unless it's a scene of scenes, one that sets your adrenaline to perking. Of the many master scene cards you've sketched out in detail, which excites you the most? That's the place to begin.

> **Cardinal Rule #21:** Write your favorite master scene first. After you've revised that scene, choose your next favorite master scene. And so on, until you've written an entire first draft of your novel as master scenes.

## *The whys of writing your novel's first draft in master scenes*

**Prevents overwriting.** Think about it. If you begin stringing beads, that is, writing the first master scene, then a minor scene, then some narrative followed by another minor scene, then a major scene before getting to the second master scene, and so on, you might well reach 80,000 words before you're halfway through your master scenes. At that point you'll find yourself projecting a novel of 160,000 words or more, an unsalable proposition for a first novelist. Where do you go from there? Write 80,000 more words and cut the finished draft in half? Or cut the first half in two and write the second half in a newly economical style? A tough proposition either way, and a monumental investment of time and effort.

**Maintains focus.** If you write only master scenes on a first draft, you will remain true to the continuity of your story, thus avoiding one of the deepest pitfalls of beginning writers: going off on tangents.

**Sustains your enthusiasm.** Don't immerse yourself in writing narrative and minor scenes transporting characters from one situation to another. You'll wish you were already at the next scene where the heroine confronts her husband with her discovery of his affair and breaks his jaw in a fistfight. If you find yourself in such a predicament, stop, drop what you're doing and roll ahead to where you want to be. If the writing is not fun for you, the person who invented this novel, imagine how it's going to feel to the reader.

**Minimizes writing stuff people skip.** Think about those jokes that go: "So the salesgirl goes to the second farmhouse and . . . " Doesn't it drive you nuts when the setup of the joke gets repeated at farmhouse after farmhouse? Don't you find yourself mentally windmilling your hands in front of the joke teller's face? Don't you just want to scream, "Get to the punch line"? Good advice. Forget the elaborate, repetitive mechanics of a setup. Write one best punch line (master scene) after another. The transitional mechanics will take care of themselves after your first draft is complete.

**Sets up transitions, tiebacks and motivations.** For example, you write your fifth master scene and realize that your heroic character has inherited a herd of llamas without ever establishing how his favorite Peruvian uncle has died (or even that he *had* an uncle living in the Andes). No problem. Make a note of it and go on to write your sixth favorite master scene. Worry about creating and terminating the uncle later.

## STEP 2: CREATE A STACK OF FIX CARDS

Simplest step in the process of writing a novel. Just keep a stack of blank 3″×5″ cards handy. When a brilliant idea occurs to you in the writing of a master scene, make a note to yourself, as in: "Fix—Explain how the uncle and his llamas came to be." Keep stacking cards as you go along. I'll tell you when and how to use your fix cards later.

You want to change your hero's eyes from blue to brown? No problem. First change the entry on the character card in your fingertip character portfolio. Then create a fix card to the effect: "Fix—Change Audie's eyes from blue to brown in the first half of the manuscript."

> **Cardinal Rule #22:** No matter what form of concordance you employ, always use fix cards. Fix cards will clear your mind of mechanical trivialities, leaving it free to concentrate on the act of creation.

Do *not* stop writing your first draft to piddle around with such trifling changes, even if your computer's writing program is equipped with a global change feature. Keep up your writing momentum by using fix cards. Caution: Do not rely on making a note to yourself in the manuscript because a fix might require changes in several spots. Make the note *and* create a fix card before moving on.

## STEP 3: CHOOSE A POINT OF VIEW

Decide whose voice will be telling the story and whose minds will be open to readers. Throughout this book, for instance, you know who's talking to you—a dogmatic, bossy writing coach. As such I'm going to make this decision easy for you by saying, in effect: Do it my way.

---

**Cardinal Rule #23:** Use a third-person, past-tense point of view (POV), and limit the novel's omniscience to your master characters.

---

A brief English 101 refresher is in order. First person is the *I, we, us* narrator. I've used it a lot in this book—in this sentence, in fact. In a first-person narration, one character tells the story and a reader can only know what goes on in that character's mind and the action on stage can occur only when the *I* narrator is present. Unless you're an accomplished writer already, don't use first-person narration. Maybe in your second or third novel.

This book uses second person even more than first person: "You know what I'm saying, right? Get it?"

Both those questions are forms of second person, the *you* is either stated or implied in the form of addressing a reader. I'm not going to go into detail. Don't even *think* about using second-person narration in your first novel—any novel, for that matter.

A third-person point of view involves a storyteller, the author, who tells what happened, usually as it happened. The third-person narrator constructs sentences like this:

> Janice Clement never imagined it was possible for her—or any woman—to have a son twenty years older than she, until a grizzled codger showed up at the door and announced himself.
>
> "Hello, Mother," he said, licking a spot of foam from one corner of his drooping mouth.

She knew all about dementia in the elderly and suppressed a giggle beneath a smile of forced civility. "What did you say?"

"I said I'm your son."

Hell with civility. This was too weird. She slammed and locked the door and went to the phone. Hesitating, she tapped the receiver against her forehead: *Call the cops or the old folks' home?* The chimes sounded again, followed by a fist pounding on the door. He was bellowing now, spewing obscenities.

*Cops. Definitely cops.*

Never mind the impossibility of the situation posed in the narrative. Just notice the point of view.

## *Salient features of the POV construction*

**Third person.** The storyteller tells using *he, she, they, them, it* terms: "*Janice* never imagined"; "*He* said"; "*She* suppressed"; "*She* slammed."

**Past tense.** These are actions and thoughts told as if they have already happened: "Janice never *imagined*"; "He *said*"; "She *suppressed*"; "She *slammed*." Even so, a sense of immediacy is not sacrificed in the telling. Especially when certain dramatic constructions are used, as in "Hesitating, she tapped the receiver against her forehead" and throughout the rest of the passage. You can see the images and feel a tension, right? That's immediacy. What's more, you get a sense of omniscience.

**The narrator's (storyteller's) limited omniscience.** You know what Janice has imagined in the past, you learn that she knows something about dementia, you see her suppressing rudeness and you can read her thoughts, in italics, as she wrestles with a decision. Going into thoughts and motives, that's omniscience—a power reserved to the gods and writers like yourself.

Yet it's a limited power in this example. Going into the codger's head to get to his thoughts and motives might well diminish this scene by eliminating some of the mystery posed by it.

The idea of limited omniscience—not going into the head of every character—doesn't prevent you, the storyteller, from visiting scene locations where none of the master characters are present. You can write a powerful action scene, entire battles, if you want. You just wouldn't be eavesdropping on the thoughts of the characters, only relaying their words and chronicling their actions.

I grant you, cardinal rule number twenty-three demands a lot without justifying much. I can't stop you from using a mix of first and third person, present tense and unlimited omniscience. You and I both have read and enjoyed these very techniques used all the time by award-winning, best-selling authors. All I can say is, you have a steep enough climb ahead of you in trying to write and sell a first novel. Why complicate the task by dabbling in experimental or, at the very least, advanced techniques before you've mastered the fundamentals?

Whether you take my advice or not, you're ready to rumble on your novel.

## STEP 4: DO ONE FINAL EXERCISE
## BEFORE WRITING YOUR NOVEL

Try this technique for learning to write like the masters:

> **Cardinal Rule #24:** Study best-selling writing by copying selected segments of your favorite best-selling author's novel word for word.

I once met an adman, Marion Kopmeyer, who told me how he learned to write advertising copy when he was in high school. He taught himself at a cost of a nickel a week by buying the *Saturday Evening Post* magazine (when it was a weekly) and laboriously handwriting every word of every advertisement from cover to cover. He landed a job in an ad agency before he finished high school, and eventually he owned his own ad business.

I wondered whether the technique could be used to write fiction. After all, it's common practice for handbooks to recommend studying successful novelists. We usually take this to mean reading their novels. Or attending formal class lectures in a literature course, usually preoccupied with themes and symbols. Seldom do you find a well-led discussion of the mechanics of writing that works, showing the hows and whys of good writing.

That's where rule twenty-four comes in. I tested the technique by both handwriting and typing segments of Larry McMurtry's *Lonesome Dove* verbatim. My conclusion: As a method of studying writing, I have found none better. It works. It will teach more about professional, salable writing than any three college courses or any five writing handbooks.

Expecting you to follow cardinal rule number twenty-four from cover to cover of an entire novel is unrealistic. As I've said, I didn't copy all of *Lonesome Dove* myself. Here are a few lessons you can learn.

**Master simple mechanics.** For instance, do you know how to punctuate dialogue? You can examine these rules at work in published novels when you copy a best-seller. Trust me, it's so much more effective and enjoyable than dragging out a grammar primer and looking up punctuation rules.

**Learn publishing conventions of the genre.** This exercise will teach you mundane stuff such as establishing chapter length and handling scene changes with narration. If you're copying a novel of the type you want to write (and, if not, why not?), you'll get a feel for how a story is structured within that category, whether the publisher allows page after page of narration and description or whether action and dialogue carry 90 percent of the novel. Important stuff to know. If you're planning to write a military techno-thriller and haven't read at least a half dozen Tom Clancy novels and copied a few passages, you're whacking at the keyboard with both hands tied behind your back.

**Create images.** Some best-selling novelists write excruciating detail to describe characters and settings. In these novels, the texture of the setting and background is every bit as important as the action. Other novelists sketch effective images with the slash of a few words. Which type of novelist are you? Find a model novel or two, and copy selected passages of imagery.

**Write effective dialogue.** A bit later I'll be giving you my short course on writing good dialogue, but nothing can teach you like copying dialogue of one of the masters. You say you want to write spare dialogue, packing it with power and meaning, tingeing it with irony and creating a sense of reality by communicating with words not said? Or even *written*? Take a page from Elmore Leonard. Literally. Open any of his novels and find a page of dialogue. Copy. Learn.

**Build scenes.** How does a best-selling novelist get the most out of her master scenes? What does Mary McGarry Morris do to position and motivate characters within a scene? How does she paint in the setting? Develop character? Move the central story line forward? Wring conflict? Create suspense? Touch the emotions? Engage the reader? Copy one of her master scenes and see for yourself.

**Economize on your novel's first draft.** This is a bottom-line payoff to writing your novel. I'm not one of those writing coaches who recommends spilling 300,000 words into an aimless first draft and then sorting out the mess during the revision process. That's why I recommend writing master scenes first—you get the central story under control and keep a tight rein on subplots and minor scenes. When you copy finished writing, you're modeling the best work a writer, her editors and her proofreaders can produce. You're not finding pet phrases and clichés repeated as they are in careless first drafts. Sentences do not run on aimlessly. You get a feel of deliberate pace, word choice and thoughtful artwork in the construction and placement of sentences, paragraphs and scenes. Do this exercise long enough and you experience a kind of existential insight as to how every word serves a purpose in a best-seller, carrying the freight of the story without diversions or tangents. In short, you learn how not to waste your own time and words.

## Considerations when copying a best-seller

**Be wary of plagiarism.** Of course you can't sell the words of another person. This exercise should help you master the *techniques* of the masters, not the exact words.

**Don't transcribe mindlessly.** This exercise mustn't feel like numbly writing on the chalkboard a thousand times "I will not run in the hallways." Instead, you should ask questions. Why did the writer use this word and that sentence fragment? Why break this cardinal rule or that rule of punctuation? And so on.

**Keep a set of cards handy.** As you're going along, you'll have one writing insight after another. Make fix cards of ideas and techniques you'll want to incorporate into your novel.

**Don't copy an entire novel at once.** If you want to write breathless action like Dean Koontz's in your climactic scene, select one of his novels and copy a suspenseful scene. Then write your own climax. Need your character to develop a distinctive identity? Pick up an Anne Tyler novel and follow one of her creations for a few scenes, copying every word she wrote about him.

Time for you to select that master scene card for the place in you own novel where you want to begin writing. Find a published best-seller you want to emulate. Open to a page where there's a similar master scene. Copy the best-seller passage. Then transfer the lessons you learned to writing your own scene.

One more step before you begin writing your own master scene.

## STEP 5: AVOID BLUNDERS THAT BRAND YOU AN AMATEUR

I've this list. I call it Ten Bumper Stickers That Cry Out "I'm an Amateur." The list is a compilation of mistakes, not including misspellings and typos, of content and structural errors many beginning writers make. Avoid them and you'll have a step up on all the first novelists who haven't this book to coach them along. Paraphrasing Jeff Foxworthy's popular comedy routine, here goes.

### YOU MIGHT BE AN AMATEUR IF . . .
### *You write endless synonyms for* said

Perhaps you've seen (or written) lines of dialogue such as these:

> "You're an animal," she said.
> "Am not," he replied.
> "Are too," she countered.
> "Oh yeah?" he challenged.
> "Yes. A pig," she added.
> "Am not," he sneered.
> "Are too," she continued.
> "A pig?" he grinned. "Really?"
> "A *fat* pig," she emphasized.

When you copy your chosen best-seller, I'll wager you never find such instances of dialogue. The pro does not write like that. She understands that *said* is an invisible word. If the context does not tell a reader who is speaking, and especially when three or more characters engage in dialogue, *said* does the job without becoming intrusive. Avoid this blunder and the next one in your quotable exchanges.

### *Your characters* sneer, grin *and* laugh *their words*

Avoid constructions that appear in the previous sample dialogue. It makes no more sense to write " 'Am not,' he jogged," than to write "he sneered." If you must indulge in a sneer, write a separate sentence, something like: " 'Am not.' He sneered at her, inviting a comeback as witty as his own."

## You use countless -ly words

Usually called adverbs, these words rarely carry a story line authoritatively. The amateur author severely taxes her brain, striving earnestly to write professionally, only to find herself crying softly, "One rejection after another." Avoid -ly constructions by finding a precise verb that expresses your meaning. Instead of *crying softly*, write *whimpering*. Try eliminating the -ly word altogether. In this very paragraph you could strengthen the material by deleting *severely*, *earnestly* and *softly*, although *usually*, *rarely* and *professionally* would have to stay to pinpoint the meaning I intended.

## You overuse adjectives

Piling on adjectives won't strengthen your writing but weaken it.

**Don't use adjectives redundantly.** Calling a diamond *white*, *hard*, *sparkling* and *valuable* adds nothing but words. The meaning is not improved because the concept of *diamond* includes all those adjectives. If the diamond is either *black*, *soft*, *dull* or *worthless*, by all means those adjectives add weight in that they contrast with the accepted notion of a diamond. Unless you mean *lump of coal*. In which case, you're back where you began.

**Don't use worthless adjectives.** James Thurber on the subject of worthless adjectives: " 'There's that goddam *pretty* again,' Ross would say. The easy overuse of *pretty* and *little* exacerbated his uneasy mind. Once, to bedevil him, I used them both in a single sentence . . . : 'The building is pretty ugly and a little big for its surroundings.' "

*Little*, *large*, *pretty* and even *beautiful* are worthless. They're as lazy and imprecise as the people who use them. Think about it. What is a little stone? Why it's a *pebble*, of course. Littler? Fine. Give it an exact dimension, say, three millimeters. That's little enough, unless you find it in your chowder or your kidney.

The final words on adverbs and adjectives: Of course you can use them in your writing but be precise and deliberate. Try using verbs and nouns first.

> **Cardinal Rule #25:** Always try using verbs and nouns before resorting to adjectives and adverbs. A concrete noun partnered with a precise verb will kick butt on adjectives and adverbs any day of the week.

### You use weasel words

*Almost, about, appears, approximately, probably, seems, greenish* (all *-ish* constructions, in fact), *halfway* and *nearly* are examples of weasel words when you rely on them instead of expending the effort to be precise. For instance, can you find anything to redeem an expression like "He almost exploded"? Do you mean he "seethed"? That he stifled his anger? Instead of halfway angry, do you mean annoyed? Irritated? Riled? Be somewhat exact about it, OK?

### You write in office language

"At this point in time"? "In order to effect meaningful change"? Only a bureaucrat writes like that. Don't you. Sure, sure, you may have characters who talk like bureaucrats. Still. Be careful. It's no saving grace to blame a bored reader on a boring character.

### You rely on clichés

This item is obligatory for any writing handbook. Beware the automatic phrase, such as "white as snow" and "quiet as a mouse." If your heroic character roars like a lion, she'd better be a lioness.

### You write dialect

'Nuff's arready bin sed on that there isshew.

### You repeat yourself over and over

Even the pros get stuck on their pet phrases. I'll bet the word *inexorable* appears a dozen times in Michael Crichton's *The Lost World*, when no novel ought to feature it more than once. Worse yet is to repeat plot information. For instance, a wife's infidelity might appear as a master scene played out in some detail. If she later is struck by guilt and finds she must explain herself to her husband, there's little point in repeating much of anything that the reader already knows. If the husband asks, "What happened?" you might write "She told him, glossing over the graphic parts." If, when she's finished, the stunned husband asks, "But why?" you can add new information, enlarging the plot problem without being redundant. If later yet, the husband finds himself explaining to his attorney why to file for divorce, there's no need repeating anything but the sketchiest of detail. Trust the reader not to forget, and move on, please.

### *You're just too precious*

Number ten in the list of amateur mistakes might be the worst, a mortal sin that covers a multitude of venial ones. I doubt anything could cause an editor to reject your manuscript faster than for you to be cute or coy. The following are signs you may be too precious in your manuscript.

**Using language and predicaments right out of sitcoms,** movies or even the day's news.

**Being playful with famous names** (Jay Letterman and David Leno?).

**Writing annoying gimmicks,** such as admittedly awful alliteration—a series of words that begin with the same letter. And add to this the practice of starting every other sentence with *but* or *and*. But also avoid using weird punctuation like multiple exclamation points!!

**Writing experimentally.** If your novel sounds like poetry, it's probably not *good* poetry. Or good prose, either.

**Using cute quote marks.** As in "She was a karate expert, a real 'knock-out.' " See what's at work there? The author is winking at you from behind the narrative, telling you he's made a funny, wanting you to notice it. Take off the quotes, and the irony is still there. Let the readers apply their own standards to how funny it is. Stick to using quote marks exclusively to fence in your dialogue.

**Stepping into the story.** The reason this device is so funny in Woody Allen movies is because it's so outrageous. But don't write expressions in which the author intrudes in the fictional world: "If she only knew what was waiting for her on the other side of that door"; and "he was wrong"; or "little did she know."

## STEP 6: BUILD SKILLS THAT DEVELOP YOUR OWN STYLE

What is style? Why, it's you, of course. Style expresses how you organize and communicate in writing. You are distinctive in a thousand different ways, from your fingerprints to your hair growth (or loss) patterns, your speech, your eating habits, your sense of humor and your inimitable take on the world. You establish a personal style when—however selfish this sounds—you shut out all concerns about what others think (including me) and tell a story that pleases you.

---

**Cardinal Rule #26:** Write to suit yourself.

---

Your audience is you and not Aunt Effie or half-a-million-plus divorced women eighteen to twenty-four years old. You stake out a distinctive style of writing to satisfy you and you alone.

That's the philosophical part. Practically speaking, your style comes through in the way you handle the following aspects of writing that first and favorite master scene.

## The elements of your style
- Writing well-paced action
- Writing effective dialogue
- Creating powerful imagery
- Crafting tiebacks and transitions

I've listed each of these elements in a rough order of their importance to the development of your style as a novelist. Let's look at each as a step in the process of writing that first master scene.

## STEP 7: DEVELOP STYLE BY WRITING WELL-PACED ACTION

Novels must move on every page, in every scene, in all your sentences, and if it's not too much to ask, they must move forward to your climactic scene. This principle applies to every category of fiction from romance to mystery to epic to western. The best writers sweep you up in the current of a moving story and pull you along like a relentless river. Even narrative passages create a sense of motion. The first principle of effective style, implied by my first cardinal rule, is explicit in rule twenty-seven.

By action I don't mean fistfights and violence. Characters need not run around shrieking. Think of it as filming a motion picture with your words rather than painting a still life in oils. Action doesn't even require people to move. Sometimes in film, the camera moves while the actors and landscape remain motionless. Sometimes a man is most compelling when he sits remembering, tears welling in his eyes.

---

**Cardinal Rule #27:** Build action into every scene, every passage of dialogue, every sentence of your novel. When in doubt, use action.

---

We've already looked at the grand-scale pacing of novels, which is achieved either by crowding master scenes or by spacing them farther apart. Now let's look at ways to increase small-scale pace and to build action into scenes, paragraphs and sentences.

## How to increase the pace of your writing
### Create white space on the page
This device is not as artificial as it sounds. A dense, gray page of type with long paragraphs seems impenetrable, like a thicket of brambles. In contrast, a page with many short paragraphs reads fast, increases the pace and heightens the sense of action. If a reader can breeze through a page of your novel, she feels the novel is moving fast for no other reason than she is able to read it quickly.

Can you get away with chopping a boring paragraph into ten to make it interesting? Nope, the action in those paragraphs must match the breaks you make.

### Write short sentences
An artful, complex, well-textured sentence crafted with shades of nuance and degrees of vigor invites a reader to absorb it, examine it, even dissect and reread it; whereas snappy, terse sentences cause the eyes to race. Again, you can't play tricks. You can't improve a long, boring sentence by breaking it into three short, boring sentences.

### Use fragments, but judiciously
Sentence fragments give the impression of immediate thoughts. In tense situations, fragments indicate excitement. Even panic. Fragments can pick up the pace of any scene. If not overused. As here.

### Choose familiar words
Look at *inexorable*. Five syllables for a word almost never spoken by most people. Uncommon, in fact, except in Michael Crichton novels.

People stumble on words like that. They inexorably slow the pace of a novel. Look what happens when you choose a four-syllable word to replace it: *implacable*. A bit more familiar and easier to read, although no more effective. Try three syllables: *relentless*. Two: *fated*. One: *grim*. Of these, I like *relentless*, don't you? Don't get the idea I'm suggesting you write a "Run, Spot, run" novel. I'm saying that you quicken pace with familiar words, as opposed to language readers might never see except in the vocabulary sections of aptitude tests.

### Exploit power words

No two words in English are precise synonyms. Take the adjective *fat*, for example. Compare it to *obese, overweight, stout, corpulent, chubby, lumpy, beefy, brawny, big-boned* and *lard-butt*. Each is tinted with different shades of meaning, some more powerful than others. Which word you use will depend on who's speaking it. A medical character might say *obese* or *overweight*. A wife would describe hubby using any one of them, depending on her mood, and you can bet she wouldn't choose *big-boned* if she was angry with him. Why? It wouldn't express her anger precisely. Always choose the most powerful word to suit a situation. You'll increase the pace of the novel.

### Never repeat information

If you're a teacher, coach or professional speaker, beware. All your career you've practiced the three-step method of (1) Tell them what you're going to tell them; (2) tell them; and (3) tell them what you told them. Abandon this practice in writing your novel. What's helpful to listeners, who can't turn back in your lecture, is offensive to readers, who can.

## *How to pump up action in the first scene you write*
### Incorporate conflict to elevate action

Conflict results when two characters want the same thing. Or when one opposes the other's goal. Or when outside forces become obstacles to your heroic character's achievement of his worthy goal.

Conflict invites full-blown action. Conflict sets the pulse of your readers' racing. Conflict keeps a novel moving. Conflict is the one indispensable ingredient in every best-seller—even the Bible would be a flop without its endless, fundamental conflict between the forces of good and evil. That's why I give you . . .

> **Cardinal Rule #28:** Capitalize on conflict. Assert it in every scene of your novel, never allowing it to fall below a discernible level of tension.

Here's a scale to show the degrees of conflict you might employ to keep the action level up.

Subsurface Tension is 1 ⟶ 10 is Frenetic Combat

Never set the throttle of your novel to cruise on placid seas. If you're not incorporating a full-blown typhoon, you ought to at least be painting an ominous cloud. If you're ever tempted to spend a few pages of your novel reveling under clear skies, don't. Incorporate a suspicious ripple that might mean a great white shark lurking beneath the surface or a tsunami building over the horizon. Otherwise, people will be skipping those pages. Conflict moves a novel because readers relish a battle, even a small one—heck, even an imagined one.

How else do you explain the audience for shock radio, combative political interviews and TV magazines? What's the common denominator in every successful television show, whether a comedy or a drama?

Conflict, of course. You think *Seinfeld* would be funny if everybody got along? Nope. The only times the characters on that show cooperate are times when they're organizing a conflict with others or racing toward an inevitable showdown of their own. It's the conflict, ma'am, the conflict that makes a hit a hit. Without it, you might as well be writing a dictionary.

I won't address the obvious methods of pumping up conflict. If you don't realize that a lovers' spat, a court confrontation, a car chase and a shoot-out are examples of overt conflict, you need more help than this book can give you.

More likely you want to advance your skill at building conflict into a static scene. Let's try it.

Here's some raw material from my novel *Cottage 13*:

A bare, gray classroom, 15 feet by 30 feet, in the maximum security lockup of a juvenile detention facility. Fluorescent lighting. The west windows look out on a rec yard. The east windows reveal the hallway of a cellblock.

What could be more static than an empty room? Let's experiment with ways of creating conflict within it.

## Techniques for incorporating conflict in your first scene

**Compare a static scene to an active one.** Use verbs and verb forms.

This was a classroom? Add some clanging bars and scowling faces, and it'd be no different than the cellblock across the hall.

**Contrast.**

Not exactly the teaching heaven he'd seen in this month's *Modern Educator* magazine. No computers. No projection televisions. No budget. No hope.

**Offend the senses.**

. . . stale, dank air—even the light was repugnant, yellow and warped through the film on the windows.

**Establish a point of view.** See through the character's eyes.

Outside he could see the rec yard, its fence topped with razor wire. Beyond its coils lay the hills, the sea, freedom. If only he could get them to see that far.

**Use a spoken point of view.**

"What do you think?" the sergeant asked.

"Stinks."

"Grim all right. Maybe you could work with it. Coat of paint. Couple posters."

"I mean the air. It stinks. Literally."

**Make it an issue of dispute.**

"I'll spruce it up. Maybe a coat of paint. Something beige or tan."

"Leave it gray," the warden said. "I don't want them forgetting they're in jail. You can't have them start liking it here."

**Hitchhike on action.**

He pinned the kid against the wall and watched his color change from lifeless gray that matched the paint to strobing blotches of purple.

**Plant a seed of mystery or foreshadow a problem.**

Lamar vowed to make this class different from the last one. Different paint, different kids, oh yeah, different outcome.

**Flash back or visualize.**

His last classroom, the one he'd been fired from, had been this barren once. He'd brought in posters, plants, and a piano. He'd brought life to it with pulsating walls and singing children. And a principal who hated his guts.

## Use active voice in all your master scenes to increase pace

A quick grammar primer: When the subject of a sentence performs the action, that is *active voice*.

*Rhonda ate the spider.*

*Rhonda* is the subject of the sentence, the eater, and *ate* is the verb, or action word. In contrast, when the subject of a sentence is the receiver of the action, that is *passive voice*.

*The spider was eaten by Rhonda.*

As before, *Rhonda* is the eat*er*, but she is no longer the subject of the sentence. That's reserved to the eat*ee*, the spider.

Quick grammar quiz. Active or passive voice?

*The spider ate Rhonda.*

If you chose active voice, congratulations.

Active voice uses fewer words than passive. It imparts a sense of immediacy. It identifies the actor performing the action.

By no means am I suggesting you can't use passive voice. Just as the active voice elevates action, the passive mellows a scene or sets up action to come. Two examples—using the classroom again. First the mellowing of a scene:

Lamar was overcome by the sheer bleakness of the room, by the gray walls, the flat, green light, the warped windows. As if he were standing inside his own soul looking out.

Second, to set up action:

> He was hit with a rush of sensations, quick pulse, hot skin, trembling muscles. His body was being mobilized. By rage. *Not again.*

## Select active words to heighten action in your first scene
Remember to use:
- concrete nouns
- action verbs
- precise adjectives used sparingly
- rare adverbs—those that cannot be eliminated
- no weasel words

Of the two selections below, which conveys more action? This?

> She was so hungry she proceeded to eat very quickly and topped it off with a couple cold ones, Coors—the only beer she'd imbibe. When she had polished off the greasy, unhealthy meal of pork, she almost felt she would burst. In point of fact, she did become ill. She blew chunks, almost getting it all over herself.

Or this selection, using the same number of words?

> She wolfed a baked potato in three bites—no chewing— and gnawed four chops to the bone, fat and all. All grunts and slurps she chugged one Coors, then another. As she crushed the second can in her greasy fist, she doubled over in full-body spasms. The meal splattered in a pool of chunks between her bare feet.

A brief dissection of the material should serve as a spotlight to the issues involved in creating action.

*She was so hungry . . .*

This is the writer *telling* you something about the character. Adding the adverb *so*, emphasizing the point, is too lame to debate. The *action* in the second selection *shows* you just how hungry the woman is, using verbs like *wolfed*, *gnawed* and *chugged*. Implied action and clear images grow out of words formed from verbs, words such as *baked, bites, chewing, grunts* and *slurps*.

    *. . . she proceeded to . . .*

An abomination. Never use this construction. Not only is it a waste of words that take up space between a subject and a verb, it also shows a tendency of the author to sound pedantic. Intentionally so.

    *. . . eat very quickly . . .*

Don't use *very* this way. *Very* points the finger at a writer straining to heighten intensity, a writer too lazy to look up a precise verb. That leaves *eat quickly*. Why not *gobble, scarf, bolt* or *wolf?*

    *. . . topped it off with a couple cold ones . . . polished off . . .*

Not so terrible but too informal—unless the narrator is consistently informal—and imprecise besides.

    *. . . the only beer she'd imbibe . . .*

*Imbibe?* Come on.

    *. . . greasy, unhealthy meal of pork . . .*

The author is telling you *he's* the health nut, more so than the character. Anyhow, it's never a good idea even for characters to preach, either to other characters or to readers. And another thing, the author is *telling* you again rather than showing. Who doesn't know pork produces grease? Contrast it with the same adjective in the second selection. A *greasy fist* is the *result* of eating with your fingers—it's an image created, not a narrative declaration.

    *. . . In point of fact . . .*

Office language.

    *. . . she did become ill . . .*

Such an innocent phrase replete with sins: vague, redundant, to *blew chunks* and euphemistic.

    *. . . She blew chunks . . .*

Better than the previous segment because at least it creates an image, but too informal, right out of *Wayne's World*.

    *. . . almost getting it all over herself.*

Weasel.

## STEP 8: DEVELOP STYLE BY WRITING EFFECTIVE DIALOGUE

Dialogue will make or break your novel. Effective dialogue cannot be faked. It works or it doesn't. And it's so easy to check out. An editor or agent can flip to a page in your sample chapters and read any dialogue selection. If it's boring, pointless puff, you're busted.

Dialogue exchanges offer some of the best opportunities for action and conflict. Follow a few simple principles and even the very first scene you write can look professional.

## Principles and pitfalls of using dialogue
### Use dialogue in all your master scenes
Such scenes are far too important to leave the inherent action and conflict to a narrator droning on. Let the characters enrich these invaluable scenes through dramatic exchanges.

### Where you see conflict, exploit it with dialogue
As you hear the narrator in your head describing conflict anywhere on the scale from mere tension to frenetic combat, ask yourself if you can use dialogue to heighten the conflict.

### Always incorporate conflict into your dialogue exchanges
If your characters aren't quarreling, at least show them in disagreement—even if it's merely a passive-aggressive attitude on the part of one character and the other isn't aware of it. If a character is alone in a scene, permit her to carry on a running argument with herself. Your first step in boredom avoidance is

> **Cardinal Rule #29:** If a line of dialogue doesn't indicate conflict or isn't leading up to conflict, don't bother writing it. Use some other narrative device.

Study this brief dialogue exchange. Find its flaws and get ready to apply a few new principles.

> "I'm concerned about you," she said.
> "Why?" he grinned ironically.
> "You haven't been yourself lately," she added.
> "Whose fault is that?" he smirked.
> She continued, "Is it mine, do you think?"
> "Yes!" he snorted. "You made me lose Vicky."
> "Oh, no," she argued. "You're wrong!"

If you've been a good student, you should have caught the attributions *added* and *continued*. They're unnecessary synonyms for *said*. I'd expect you also to identify the words *smirked* and *grinned* as body language that cannot be verbalized. If you accept *snorted*, I invite you to try snorting the word *yes*. Would you like to reconsider?

But, hey, that's routine stuff. The real problem with this passage? The exchange is flat. The writer missed chances to heighten the conflict and incorporate action. Let's revise using the principles that follow.

### Dialogue exchanges invite action—*capitalize*

Here are three ways to capitalize.

**Show motion**—appropriate behaviors for the words being spoken. In the previous example, other than the lame facial expressions, you don't see any action. Contrast that to the movement written into the next scene. Curtain beads move, a voice quavers, the woman crosses the setting, puts out a hand, toys with an ear and so on.

**Show emotion** rather than using attributive helpers. Above the author writes "she argued." You often see such helpers: "she joked," "he admitted," "she said hotly." Such instances indicate nothing less than a lack of effort. The writer didn't try hard enough to write dialogue that could stand alone. So she tried to prop up a line with helping language. If somebody is joking, arguing, admitting or saying hotly, let the language inside quotes convey that meaning.

**Craft nonverbal language.** You won't find any overt sexual proposition in the passage below, but the woman's touching in combination with the spoken words suggests one. What's more, the boy in the story carries on his side of the conversation twice without saying a word. Once he raises an eyebrow, accepted as an expression of a question. Next he turns his back on her, and you know what that means. Examine this revision:

> The curtain beads made the clicking of a rosary. "What are you doing in my bedroom?" he asked, hating the quaver in his voice.
>
> She crossed the threadbare rug, looked up into his downcast eyes, and put a hand on his shoulder. "I'm concerned about you." One finger toyed with the fuzz on his ear. Droplets of sweat dotted her upper lip. "I wanna help is all."

"Don't bother." He shrugged off the hand. "I already got a mom."

"All this hostility. Where is it coming from, honey?"

He raised an eyebrow at her.

"Me? You think I'm to blame for your troubles with Vicky?"

"As if you didn't know."

"She's just a child, hon. Now me, I'm a real woman."

He turned away from her.

"You're wrong, momma's boy," she said to his back, "wrong as hell. You were scared of Vicky and now you're scared of me, too. That's it, isn't it? You aren't hostile; you're scared. Scared of all women but your momma." She stormed out, whipping the beadwork curtain aside. One string broke.

He heard glass beads rolling between the rumples of the kitchen linoleum long after she'd tramped across the sagging porch and disappeared into the sopping night. Or was that the sound of the truth of her accusation careening around inside his head?

What can we learn from this revision?

## Use dialogue exchanges to move the story line forward

The revision is replete with underlying tension and overt conflict. You hear the clicking of rosary beads preceding a bedroom proposition. You see movement toward a larger showdown. You see poverty, gender anxiety. You learn of a history of trouble between the young man and Vicky. You know you've not seen the last of troubles between these two characters. If a scene is written properly, you feel a tiny bit smug that you know its history, and you're eager to read ahead to see the outcome. Use dialogue to introduce problems, expand upon them or solve them in part—that's moving a story line forward.

Caution: Don't tag every line of dialogue with action, behaviors, thoughts and attributions—let dialogue find its own momentum where characters play off each other's words. This is most important as conflict builds, emotions flare and the pace quickens in a scene.

## Pick up the pace in dialogue

**Write snappy exchanges.** Let your characters use contractions and fragments. Let them bark at each other once in a while. You can't write explanatory patter, slap on quotes and call it dialogue.

**Break up long passages.** Use two or three exchanges instead of one long dialogue passage.

**Establish a rhythm.** The boy speaks, the woman responds, the boy shoots back, she asks a question, he responds, the woman puts him down. And cruelly.

### Use dialogue exchanges to characterize

Without ever saying so, the passage above suggests youth and sexual uncertainty in the boy. The woman comes off as bolder, more mature and not a little vindictive. You don't have to write an entire biography into every dialogue exchange, but you ought to at least add a few details of texture in rounding out your characters. She looking up into his downcast eyes tells you two things: He's embarrassed and the taller of the two. When this scene ends, we know how uncertain he is.

### Use dialogue exchanges to create atmosphere

The beaded curtain, the shack, the threadbare rug, droplets of sweat, rumpled linoleum and a bedroom off the kitchen—these details establish a setting without writing a hundred words of description. The beads of sweat, the sopping night. Is this setting Alaska in winter or Mississippi any time of year?

### Let punctuation signal a change of speakers

With two speakers, you won't have to identify each by name or attribute every line of dialogue with *he said/she said*. A new paragraph does that when it begins with the double quotes.

In lengthy exchanges, have one character use the other's name or use it yourself in attribution—but don't overdo either technique. The distinctive flavor of a character's words should identify the speaker.

By the way (and I don't recommend it), if a speaker should continue one paragraph of dialogue into another without interruption, leave the closing quotes off the end of the first paragraph. Use opening quotes on the second paragraph. Close the second passage of dialogue in the normal way.

### Avoid preaching, teaching and speeching

Remember the television show *Designing Women*? Once an episode the character Julia Sugarbaker would go off, lecturing the other characters and the audience on some social issue. Shouting, ranting, boring. Her raving sermons became a staple of the show. I can't imagine a better example of what *never* to do in the dialogue—or narrative, for that matter—of a novel.

Does this mean you can never allow one character to lecture another? No, it happens all the time in good storytelling, sometimes to great effect. Take the show *Frasier*. The Doctors Crane speechify all the time, but what happens to them? They wind up looking foolish, and comically so. That's as it should be when you start writing sermons into your novel.

### Avoid small talk

Not a single word. Don't begin dialogue exchanges with three lines like this before getting to the meat of your story:

> "Hi, Bob."
> "Well, hello, Sal. Long time no see. What's happening?"
> Sal squinted, confused. "Not much. What do you want?"

As a reader, that's what I want to know. Granted, people in our world do talk like that. Not in good fiction, though (although I must confess that in the movie *Pulp Fiction*, I was mesmerized at the effectiveness of double meanings and undercurrents in the film's small talk). Better in your novel to start the same scene this way:

> Sal planted herself before Bob. "You've got thirty seconds. What's so important that it can't wait till the hockey game's over?"

As in the earlier exchange between the boy and the woman in his bedroom, just assume that all the small talk has already taken place or will never take place. Start your dialogue exchange with a suggestion of conflict. Otherwise, you'll condition readers to skip the first three or four lines of every passage of dialogue.

### STEP 9: CREATE POWERFUL IMAGERY

It's a blunder to write description. That's my attitude and the reason I think in terms of *imagery* instead of the *D*-word.

> **Cardinal Rule #30:** Rather than describe, create powerful images.

Describing suggests a verbal photograph of a static object or situation: To describe implies stopping a story to take care of housekeeping details.

In contrast, creating imagery suggests motion. Even if you see this rule as an issue of semantics, it's worth adopting because it changes your approach to handling static situations.

If you want to go beyond semantics, take a practical view. If anyone at all in the publishing business reads your writing sample, the first person to do so likely will be an intern or associate on the first rungs of the business. That means somebody young, probably in her twenties. She's a product of MTV, Jim Carrey movies, *Seinfeld*, semi-funny home videos, the Internet, point-and-click, cell phones, Sega, hockey, *USA Today*, *People*, Amazon.com and the shopping channel. She starts her day with a nonfat decaf latte and sample chapters from two equally brilliant writers. Yours is full of static description. His sings with action; even the images at rest create an impression of motion, direction, cause, effect and consequence. What is going to start this woman's pulse racing? Neither the decaf nor your pages of description. Depend on it.

How do you create images? In many ways, some artificial or mechanical, others subtle and artful.

### Tips for creating powerful imagery

**Paint the image in small bites.** Never stop your story's momentum to write long descriptive passages. Anytime you've written a third consecutive sentence of static imagery, you've crossed a line where your novel risks coming to a halt. One best-selling author of today throws on the brakes to stop the story every time she introduces a character. Even walk-ons get a full paragraph or two of description complete with wisecracking observations in the mind of the main character. When you read her books you begin to recognize the parts you can skip without losing your place in the story.

**Incorporate images into action,** as in the sample passage on dialogue: "She crossed the threadbare rug, looked up into his downcast eyes." If the narrator reveals the same information this way—"The rug on his bedroom floor was threadbare. He stood there, his eyes downcast. He was taller than her"—that's description. Static. The author's talking. Can you hear him?

**See through the character's eyes.** Hear through his ears. Feel through his skin. It isn't "Glass beads rolled in the rumples of the kitchen linoleum." It's "He heard glass beads. . . ." Get it? When you can, use the character's senses instead of the author's.

**Salt dialogue with nonintrusive images.** A quaver in a voice. That's an image. So is toying with somebody's ear, as are droplets of sweat on a lip.

**Use the tiny but telling detail.** Like the harvester ant, the smallest detail can pack a lot of freight. Rumples in the kitchen linoleum indicate water damage to the floorboards, or termites (harvester ants?), or just plain old age, wear and neglect.

**Choose action-bearing verbs.** *Toyed, stormed, tramped, whipping, careening*—these words do so much more than say what is. They indicate sensuality, anger and fear.

**Choose action-bearing nonverbs.** *Clicking* is a verb form used as a noun. *Quaver*, for example, is used as a noun, but it's also a verb in another context. "*Rumples* of . . . linoleum," "*sagging* porch," "*sopping* night." All imply action because they are forms of verbs.

**Connect to known images.** Here I'm talking about similes and metaphors without using the grammatical terms. The curtain beads made the clicking of a rosary. You don't have to be a Catholic to connect with this image. Just be careful you don't fall into the trap of clichés—"like a rattlesnake"; the commonplace—"a baby's rattle"; the colloquial— "rattled like a BB in a boxcar" (which jars the ear in the boy-woman exchange); the ridiculous—"like a cup of liar's dice"; or the obscure— "a cup of liar's dice at the Oil City Bar in Shelby, Montana."

**Invent fresh settings.** What if the woman didn't slink into the boy's bedroom? Suppose she'd crawled into a pup tent he'd put up in the backyard. The implication there borders on incest.

**Show an unusual side of commonplace settings.** Place a wall-sized, high-definition projection television screen in this shack and you create a different image.

**Show an uncommon usage of common language.** The woman didn't exit the shack into the *steamy* night. Too automatic. *Sopping* night suggests the highest possible humidity short of rain.

**Create an image without saying so.** In our example, it's a shanty. Do you doubt it?

So much for imagery. You're almost ready to begin cranking out the first draft of your first scene.

## STEP 10: CREATE TIEBACKS AND TRANSITIONS

First transitions. When you're writing, how do you keep the story in motion from one paragraph to the next, scene to scene, and chapter twelve to chapter thirteen? Any number of ways. Let's look at some.

### *How to transition*

**Use obvious transitional words and phrases.** *Later, an hour later, next morning, when summer came, soon after.* Like that. One caution: Don't get so hung up on moving readers along that you have to hold their hands. You can overuse this device. Beware.

**Reflect words and phrases.** Words in a previous segment are repeated outright in the opening of a new segment. You end a chapter with "No way around it—she'd have to compel him to talk." You open the next chapter with "She blocked his path and said, 'We have to talk.' "

**Reflect concepts and ideas.** Using the previous example, you open the next chapter with

> "She followed him into the Ritz-Carlton, then into the men's room. He saw her in the mirror, his eyes showing all the whites. Before he could open his mouth, she shoved his face into the wall. 'Start singing, creep, before I feed you the big pink mints out of the urinal.' "

**Don't.** The best way of all to get from one place to the next is just to go there and begin writing. Readers are clever enough to follow a well-written, logical story line, even one with flashbacks and detours. One of the most dreadful habits for a beginning writer to develop is to waste time and words moving people around.

Take that last example, the woman vowing to confront the man. No *next day*, no cab ride from O'Hare International Airport, no tip for the doorman, no questions for the concierge, no debating with herself about how to approach her mark. She follows the guy into the bathroom, over-powers him and threatens him. Forgive me the immodesty, but I like it.

## *How to tie back*

Transitions in reverse are tiebacks. For your novel to transcend a feeling of "this happened, then this happened, then that," you establish relationships between the action of one scene and any number of previous scenes. Here are several devices you can use.

**Cause and effect.** Easy, if you've followed all the logic to here. You establish that a character wants something (a worthy goal) and acts to get it. Why? Motivation, of course. This causes a ripple effect. In later scenes a worthy adversary throws up obstacles, creating problems. Never write so subtly that your reader can't pick up these fundamental relationships, even in a mystery.

**Logical progressions.** Your heroine will die unless she finds the antidote for the poison in her system. As the novel proceeds, so must the degree of her illness.

**Foreshadowing and planting.** We discussed this in dissecting the film *Jurassic Park*, when the paleontologist Alan Grant talked about raptors hunting in packs. Which came to pass during the climactic scenes. And remember the opening image of the fossil claw? Did you catch its reflection later in the kitchen scene when the raptor tapped its claw while hunting the grandkids?

**Artful, invisible imagery.** You can repeat yourself without seeming to. Refer to the dialogue exchange between the woman and the boy again. The rosary, sometimes called prayer beads, reflect in the sound of the beaded curtain. That's an immediate, obvious tieback. More subtle are the droplets of sweat, which are what, if not beads? Subtler yet is the notion of a rosary contrasted with a sexual situation. Finally the broken bead string and rattling bits of glass close the scene like a second bookend.

Let's see what you can do. Using all the techniques of this chapter get on with writing your first, most favorite master scene. When you're finished, don't start on your second scene yet. Revise the draft of that first scene according to principles of the next chapter.

One last thing: If you get stumped along the way, work through it. Don't reinvent the disease known as writer's block.

"To put it bluntly, writer's block is a hoax," Richard Walter writes in *Screenwriting*. "Blockage is writing's natural state. It derives from the immature notion that writing ought to be fun, ought to be easy, ought to flow like Niagara, or if not quite Niagara, like some dependable country creek."

So, no excuses.

One final thing before you begin. Using this format, create a chapter log to keep in your Writer's Tool Kit. You'll use this log continually because you've forgotten the number of the last chapter. Also you can use it to establish some kind of continuity for chapter length. Such a log was indispensable in writing this book: Without it I kept forgetting the sequence and placement of cardinal rules and figures each time I wanted to number a new one. Figure ten shows a sample you can copy onto a sheet of paper and keep in your folder.

| Chapter Log: _____ | | | | | |
|---|---|---|---|---|---|
| Chapter Number | Start Page # | End Page # | Total Pages | Chapter Title | Synopsis of Master Scenes in This Chapter |
| | | | | | |
| | | | | | |

Fig. 10. Chapter log

Meet you at chapter five when you're finished writing that draft of your first scene.

# 5 REVISE YOUR NOVEL TO BEST-SELLER STANDARDS

**35 tips for turning a workable draft into a manuscript that agents will fight over and editors will bid on**

Omit needless words. Vigorous writing is concise. A sentence should contain no unnecessary words, a paragraph no unnecessary sentences.

Strunk and White
*The Elements of Style*

Writing is way overrated. Revision counts for far more of the art in any novel. Revision is the money game, the finishing touch. What's the point of dressing your novel and sending it off to New York in a tuxedo if you've left its trouser fly unzipped?

The most important benefit to writing a scene, then revising it before going on to write a second scene, is that it's the quickest way for you to develop a professional, salable style. If you make and correct all your boneheaded mistakes in the first scene, you'll write a far better, more salable first draft of the second scene.

## MECHANICAL PRELIMINARIES

If you're writing on a computer or word processor, these preliminary steps will be done on screen. Later you'll print and revise a paper version of each scene. If you're not writing on a word processor, the best advice I can give you is find one. Libraries and schools often have labs where you can use a computer. I have written novels in longhand and finished and revised three books on typewriters. The most serious deficiency in that method is not the work you have to put in typing a manuscript three or four times; the problem is you'll tend to take shortcuts in revision to *avoid* retyping a chapter, renumbering pages and the like. If you must stick to typewriting, from here on, adapt as best you can to the advice I'll be giving to those with electronic means of writing.

## STEP 1: ADOPT A PROFESSIONAL FORMAT FOR YOUR MANUSCRIPT

Avoid boneheaded mistakes.

- **Double-space lines of type**—it's an industry standard. Never single-space, even on drafts. Forget about the economies of saving paper. You edit your work best when it's double-spaced.
- **Establish professional margins.** Use an inch and a quarter left and right and an inch at the top and bottom. On first pages of chapters, leave a third to a half page of white space.
- **Number pages** in either the upper or lower right.
- **Identify pages** in the upper left with your last name and one or more words from the title, as in "Smith—*You Can Write.*"
- **Write only on one side of the page.** Don't even make notes to yourself on the backs of pages—it's too easy to overlook them.
- **Never use any form of binding** on your manuscript. Leave it as a stack of loose pages.
- **Use standard paper**—20-pound, white, letter-size (8½″ × 11″).
- **Avoid tricky typefaces.** Use Courier, Bookman, New York and similar serif typefaces. Serif types have the "feet" and "ears" on the letters. Don't use sans serif faces such as Helvetica and Avant Garde—they're unadorned but harder to read in book-length works. And don't write long passages in italics.

## STEP 2: SPELL-CHECK YOUR SCENE

Manually or electronically.

If your software contains a grammar check, it can help you, too. Even if it becomes tedious, run it.

## STEP 3: ELIMINATE DOUBLE SPACES BETWEEN WORDS AND SENTENCES

Published novels will not contain two consecutive spaces after sentence punctuation. So eliminate those now and stop typing them into your manuscript if you've been doing so. Another common typo is the use of two spaces between words. Most word processing programs contain a global change feature that will correct this error. Allow the program to run until all occurrences of the incorrect spacing have been located and corrected.

## STEP 4: UPDATE YOUR CHARACTER PORTFOLIO
A housekeeping detail, but an essential one. Immediately after finishing your first master scene, update character cards for anyone who appeared in the scene. Enter physical and attitudinal details. Modify motivations. Identify distinctive speech patterns that must remain consistent throughout the novel.

## STEP 5: ADD NEW SCENE CARDS
Writing one scene begets ideas for new scenes. Don't trust your memory to keep track of a new plot idea. Create a new scene card, adding enough detail to guarantee you won't forget its essence, and insert it in the proper place in your card stack.

## STEP 6: MAKE THE APPROPRIATE FIXES
## TO THE DRAFT SCENE
Review your fix cards. If you find that a detail or plot twist came to mind while writing your first master scene, update your draft.

## STEP 7: CONDUCT YOUR FINAL RESEARCH
Research a novel *after* you've begun writing it? Absolutely.

Conduct only enough research to refine your story and to remain true to as many facts as you intend to. Some writers, Michael Crichton and Tom Clancy, for example, rely on research to set the central stage upon which all action is played out. But every writer will bend an inconvenient fact to suit the dramatic purpose of his story. Without getting into wrongs and rights of that, all I'm saying is, research deeply enough to use what you find to the best storytelling advantage. The alternative is to spend (or waste) time collecting details that will never get into a novel. Chances are, if you pack a novel with factual detail, you'll have to explain so much that it will get in the way of the story.

> **Cardinal Rule #31:** Research only as much as necessary to enrich your novel with reality or, even better, a sense of wonder or discovery. Never include data for its own sake or, worse, to show how brilliant you are.

## STEP 8: REWORK YOUR SCENE CARDS WITH RELEVANT RESEARCH

Before you forget, add pertinent details you learned from your research to the master scene you've written. Also jot notes on other cards in your outline stack, indicating other places you'll rely on research to develop your story line.

## STEP 9: REVIEW YOUR NUGGET STATEMENT

That summary of your story in 35 to 40 words? The one you should have prominently posted or handy in your pocket or pocketbook? Does the scene you've written remain true to the statement? If not, you risk losing your focus. Revise the scene to fit your original purpose. Unless that purpose has changed. In which case, revise both your nugget and the stack of scene cards.

## STEP 10: CHECK THE SCENE FOR FUNCTION

Reread the scene you wrote, identifying whether it fulfills the purposes indicated for it on the master scene card.

### RUN A BUG SWEEP

Here you sweep your scene, looking for and eliminating mechanical glitches that are the enemies of selling a manuscript.

## STEP 11: HUNT DOWN -*LY* WORDS AND KILL THEM

Use the "find" function of your computer, looking at every single instance of -*ly* in your scene. Evaluate adverbs one by one, according to the guidelines I gave you earlier:

- **Can it be eliminated without changing meaning?** If so, do so.
- **Is the -*ly* word trying to prop up a weak verb?** If so, find a specific power verb to carry the freight.

## STEP 12: KILL EXCLAMATION POINTS!

Find them. Assassinate them. Especially in sentences where you've tried too hard to create a sense of urgency: "The house was afire!" The punctuation doesn't add anything to the meaning of the sentence, except to point out an author's breathless, witless attempt to dramatize. Dramatize with action, not punctuation. Eliminate exclamation points, except in genuine exclamations: "Aha!"

## STEP 13: ELIMINATE BODY LANGUAGE
## VERBALIZATIONS IN DIALOGUE

Run the "Find" function again, looking for these words one by one:

| | |
|---|---|
| chuckle | snap |
| giggle | sneer |
| grin | snort |
| laugh | spat |
| smirk | titter |

When you find one used in the form of a verbal attribution (" 'No way,' he laughed"), fix it according to the guidelines I've already given you. OK, if you want to keep *titter*, grant yourself a single use in your novel but no more.

## STEP 14: EDIT SYNONYMS FOR *SAID*

Sweep your manuscript for the following:

| | | |
|---|---|---|
| added | claimed | maintained |
| admitted | commented | **queried |
| *advised | confessed | **quipped |
| *affirmed | continued | **related |
| **agreed | *declared | remarked |
| answered | emphasized | *replied |
| argued | explained | reported |
| **avowed | **joked | revealed |

When you find any of these words used to attribute dialogue, replace it with *said*. If *said* seems an inadequate substitute for a word like *joked*, it's because your line of dialogue isn't carrying the irony you intended to inject. Revise the sentence. By the way, * indicates a particularly objectionable word and ** indicates an utter abomination.

## STEP 15: ELIMINATE CLICHÉS

Run a check for *like* and *as*. See if you used them to construct a cliché, as in "quiet as a mouse" or "work like a dog." These are the obvious bugs you can fix at a stroke. Sweep for these other clichés as well:

| | |
|---|---|
| acid test | lead balloon |
| bad blood | lion's share |
| bated breath | lock, stock and barrel |
| beat a hasty retreat | name of the game |
| bit off more than he could chew | nick of time |
| boggles the mind | over a barrel |
| bound and determined | sick and tired |
| by the same token | sickening thud |
| can of worms | tail between his legs |
| dull thud | ton of bricks |
| end of her rope | toss and turn |
| end result | ulterior motive |
| fell swoop | vast wasteland |
| green with envy | (vast *anything*, in fact) |
| half the battle | vicious circle |
| hit the sack | |

Entire books have been written to list clichés, but this brief inventory covers some of the most objectionable.

## STEP 16: INVENTORY YOUR *ANDS* AND *BUTS*

At the beginning of sentences. Few editors will object if you use the device occasionally. But overusing it becomes an affectation, and bothersome besides.

## STEP 17: SWAT THE "ATOMIC FLYSWATTERS"

Theodore M. Bernstein's term for words a writer uses hopefully to inject dull writing with dramatic effect (*The Careful Writer*, Atheneum). Unless a character uses them in quotes to serve a specific dramatic intent, find these words and write them out of your narrative:

| | |
|---|---|
| amazing | divine |
| awful | dreadful |

| | |
|---|---|
| earthshaking | petrified |
| enormous | sensational |
| fabulous | stupendous |
| fantastic | super |
| frightful | terrible |
| gorgeous | tremendous |
| horrible | unbelievable |
| mad | wonderful |

## STEP 18: TERMINATE "..."

The dot-dot-dot thing can become bothersome, particularly the ".." device to indicate a pause in dialogue. Never use this technique in your novel.

## STEP 19: ELIMINATE PET WORDS AND EXPRESSIONS

Be honest. Do you find yourself using favorite phrases repeatedly? Find the first use and search for repetitions. Modify such pets so they don't crop up more than once in a manuscript. Create new expressions.

## STEP 20: CUT BIG WORDS DOWN TO SIZE

Don't be pompous. Mistrust any word five syllables or longer. Why? Because readers will think you arrogant. *Attitudinal? Institutionalize? Recapitulate?* Unless a word like that serves a dramatic purpose (a pompous character says it), don't allow the narrator to use it.

As for shorter words, they can be obnoxious, too. Don't use *initiate* when *start* will do. Same with *optimum* versus *best* and *utilize* versus *use.* Be suspicious of all words that end in *-ize* or *-ization.*

## STEP 21: ELIMINATE THE TWO BLOODSUCKERS
## WORSE THAN VAMPIRES

*There's* a bloodsucker. *It's* just as bad. Few words do more damage to a sentence, no matter how innocent they look. Find all instances where you've begun a sentence with *It is* or *It's* or *There is* or *There's.* Recast the sentence, giving it a lifesaving transfusion of action.

Instead of "There is a lion ahead. It is running at us," try "A tawny blur streaked toward us, a lion in the attack."

## STEP 22: SHUN -*ION* CONSTRUCTIONS

Another global search. Find words ending in -*ion* and see if they're part of mushy sentences: "She asked for the cooperation of the entire department but nobody accepted her recommendation for the adoption of the plan of attack." As opposed to "She asked the entire department to cooperate, but nobody accepted her plan."

## STEP 23: KILL WORDS AND PHRASES
## THAT DESERVE TO DIE

Another list. Run your scene up against words in the first column below. When you hit a match, pick an alternative from the second column.

### *Four felonies*

in order to ...............................................to
for the purpose of ....................................to
in the near future ....................................soon
in the event that ......................................if

### *And some misdemeanors*

additional .............................................added, more, other
afford an opportunity ............................allow, let
approximately ........................................about
at the present time ................................now
disseminate ...........................................issue, send out
due to the fact that ...............................due to, since
endeavor ...............................................try
expeditious ...........................................fast, quick
facilitate ...............................................ease, help
finalize .................................................complete, finish
hopefully ..............................................she hoped
impact ..................................................effect, change, hit
in conjunction with ..............................with
in regard to ..........................................about, on
pertaining to .........................................about, of, on
provide .................................................give, say, supply
retain ...................................................keep
therefore, thus ......................................so
and/or ..................................................(choose one)

him/her ...................................................(choose one)
on or about ............................................(choose one)
etc., et cetera .........................................(don't use)

## STEP 24: EDIT DOUBLETS

Edit and revise your manuscript using a little creativity and imagination to cut and eliminate words connected by *and* or *or* when such words and phrases repeat the same idea and concept without enlarging or building upon the meaning and message because they are redundant and repetitive. Get it? Separating such Siamese twins adds punch and vigor to your writing and prose. See what happens when you take a pen or pencil to this very paragraph to cut the *and*s and *or*s and half of each doublet.

Check for these abominations, too:

| | |
|---|---|
| by and by | this and that |
| so-and-so | thus and so |
| such and such | yet and still |

## STEP 25: DEAL HARSHLY WITH GNATS

Is it *its* or *it's*? Little words that slip through your screens like gnats. Even professional writers sometimes mistype them. Here's a list of bugaboos that can make you look stupid. Run a global search on each one in your completed master scene. When you find one used incorrectly, stamp it out.

## *Pesky gnats*

*Affect* as a verb means to influence. As a noun it refers to outward appearance. *Effect*, the verb, means to produce; the noun is the result produced. "Liquor affects her affect instantly, creating a bizarre effect on her face as it effects change in her behavior." Whew.

*Alot.* Wrong. Make it two words: *a lot.*

*Alright.* No, all wrong, *all right*?

*As* my journalism school professor, John Bremner, often ranted, *like* is not a conjunction. It's "He worked like a veteran, as a good boy should." Test *like* by mentally replacing it with *similar to* or *similarly to.* If it sounds right, leave *like.* If it doesn't sound sensible, the correct word is *as.* Try it in the example above.

*Blond* is applied to men, both as an adjective and a noun. "His hair is blond, so he is a blond." Women have more latitude with the adjective.

"She has either blonde hair" or "she has blond hair." But when used as a noun, "She's always a blonde." Some authorities do not distinguish between the sexes in this manner, but I rather like it.

*Entitled* refers to a rightful claim. When you put a title on your novel, you *title* it. You never *entitle* a book, a song or a poem, no matter how often you hear the term misused on radio and television.

*Farther* refers to literal distances: "He ran a mile farther." Need I say *further?*

*Fewer* is used with countables, Bremner preached, and *less than* with collective quantities. "She has fewer than ten fingers and less than enough sense."

*Imply* means to suggest. *Infer* means to deduce. "From what you imply in your accusation, I infer you'll be pressing charges against me." You'd think that just by guessing television writers would get this distinction half the time. But no, they put the wrong word into the actors' mouths every time.

*Its* is possessive, *it's* a contraction of *it is.*

*Loan* is always a noun. To *lend* money is to make a *loan.* Never let your characters *loan* money, unless you give them permission to display *their* ignorance by using the expression in dialogue.

*Their* is a possessive, *they're* a contraction, *there* a pronoun.

*Unique* doesn't allow for degrees of comparison. *More unique, most unique* and *so unique* are all incorrect.

*Your* is possessive, *you're* a contraction of *you are.*

So much for revision by using the global search function of your computer. If you follow these steps, mechanical as they are, you will have eliminated the little bugs that cry out in their tiny voices that you are an amateur. From here on out, you're going to have to work at revising some style into your novel.

## RUN A STYLE SWEEP

In contrast to the bug sweep, in which you identify mechanical glitches, this sweep guides you in developing a distinctive writing style that will catch an editor's eye.

## STEP 26: TAKE A STAND

Write decisively. You might populate your novel with the occasional wishy-washy character, and even the most heroic character suffers periods of indecision. You, as an author, cannot indulge in uncertainty.

A novelist who won't take a stand either hasn't a clear picture to communicate or is writing deliberate mush. Either way, a reader deserves to be angry.

Don't write: "He felt as if he might become ill. Gradually, he came to believe he could not quell the sickness rising from his abdomen. He thought the feeling of being nauseated would overcome him" when you mean "He threw up."

> **Cardinal Rule #32:** Take a stand. Avoid splitting hairs in images and emotions, especially in master scenes. Dramatize. Exaggerate. Embellish facts. Clarify your fictional truths.

Your duty is to transport readers into the world you're creating. To paraphrase Thoreau, clarify, clarify. Check your scene to be sure you haven't written either half emotions or fuzzy images. Every time you read a form of the words *think, perceive, conceive, seem, believe* or *feel*, an alarm should go off in your writer's brain, alerting you to rewrite the imprecisions.

Just as bad is overwriting, photographically re-creating minute details of a setting. Establish a clear impression and get on with the story. If you need further details, add them as you go. Don't drag out every burp, grunt and wheeze as a character grows angry.

Most damaging, an author sometimes can be seen working behind a scene, manipulating the puppet's strings, changing things to make the writer's job easier.

> **Cardinal Rule #33:** Once you clarify images and emotions, be consistent with the stand you've taken. Never change on whimsy or by coincidence. Once established, only the characters influenced by their realistic, competing motivations—and not the author—can reorder images and emotions.

One modern, best-selling author writes characters that spew filth at each other in one scene, then fall into bed in the next. I don't object either to spew or to bedrooms, but nothing happens between scenes that would justify a change of heart, making such behavior laughable (all the way to the bank, I suppose).

Last of all, check for intentional imprecision you've used as a way of artificially creating mystery or building suspense. To borrow from Robert Fulghum:

> **Cardinal Rule #34:** Play fair. Don't withhold details crucial to understanding the story just so you can spring a surprise later.

When you leave out necessary detail, that's cheating. Another even better selling author wrote a novel in which law enforcement principals discuss a crime at the front of the story. At the tale's end, the heroic character solves the crime with a deduction that arises directly from information given during the conference, information so basic that only a moron would not have suspected the surprise murderer from the start. This was not an insignificant detail planted and overlooked by a reader, either. If you read the book, the instant you saw the solution in print, you thumbed back to the front and asked why the heroic character didn't find the killer in the first chapter. Answer: Because the author needed to fill the space between the planted detail and the story's climax with a novel. The author cheated.

## STEP 27: GIVE MOUTH-TO-MOUTH TO DROWNING VERBS

Official writing teaches us the drowning verb syndrome. Here's an example that demonstrates: "The secret committee held a meeting to give consideration to Ambrose's plan. Committee members made the decision to give their approval to it." As opposed to "The secret committee approved Ambrose's plan." It's safe to assume the members met before bestowing their approval.

Unlike the global searches, these aren't so easy to catch. The trick is to look for the verb form that's being drowned in weak verbs, such as *give, hold, make, involve* and *is.*

## STEP 28: TEST FOR SINGULARITY

Don't ramble. Wordiness diffuses ideas. Don't juggle too many story lines at one time. Keep your reader on track throughout the story. If you get tricky and zig when he zags, you could lose him. Fact is, you could get lost yourself.

---

**Cardinal Rule #35:** Maintain singularity: one idea for each sentence; a single topic for each paragraph; a singular plot point for each scene. And stick to the main story line in writing your novel's first draft.

---

This rule isn't as hidebound as it seems. I wouldn't dream of outlawing big words, complicated sentences and richly textured scenes in complex stories. All I'm saying is even intricate sentences, paragraphs and scenes ought to keep to one point. And, of course, every scene should somehow lead to the climactic scene and the novel's logical ending. Is it too much to ask you to let the reader know where you're going?

The fixes for lapses in singularity? Simple.

- **Break violating sentences** into shorter sentences, each with a single idea, no matter how many words you use.
- **Separate rambling paragraphs** into multiple paragraphs, each with a single topic.
- **Create two scenes** when one is causing too many problems.
- **Work on subplots** only after you've finished the main story line.

## STEP 29: EDIT FOR SNAP

Crack the whip on your first draft.

---

**Cardinal Rule #36:** Achieve dramatic effect by adding snap—power words, quick pace and high emotion—to the ends of your critical sentences, paragraphs and scenes.

---

I'll illustrate by drawing from the scene where the woman enters the boy's bedroom through the beaded curtain.

**Sentences.** "The curtain beads made the clicking of a rosary. 'What are you doing in my bedroom?' he asked, hating the quaver in his voice." The emotions of hatred and fear placed at the end of the second and most important sentence punch up that sentence.

Another thing. You can add snap in degrees, depending on how directly you state it.

Direct declaration: "Hating the quaver" in the sentence above literally means "he hated the quaver." You can see how direct that is.

Reverse declaration: "Not liking the quaver" softens the phrase in two ways. Obviously, it uses a softer verb form. "I don't like you" is less confrontive than "I hate you." Besides that, the *not* construction allows a writer to combine the negative *don't* with the positive *like*. The result is ambiguity, vagueness and a dulling of the phrase's harshness. That's not necessarily bad. Sometimes ambiguity can be the writer's best friend. Just be aware of the distinction when you want to revise either to add snap or to soften a sentence.

**Paragraphs.** Placing the more powerful sentence at the end of the paragraph creates the stronger effect. Reversing the two sentences in our example will demonstrate:

> "What are you doing in my bedroom?" he asked, hating the quaver in his voice. The curtain beads behind her made the clicking of a rosary still.

**Scenes.** The strongest conflict in that scene plays out in the next-to-last paragraph where the woman berates the boy, storms out and whips the beadwork curtain aside, breaking one string of beads. The scene ends two sentences later. Imagine how the effect would be diluted by droning on for three or four more paragraphs.

**Rule of Thumb:** In scenes or narrative primarily written to relate information to the reader, put the central information at the front of the material and elaborate upon it. In scenes of high tension and conflict, pile up the action and emotion. Deliver the punch line and add snap to the end of the scene.

## STEP 30: RUN A READABILITY SCAN

Better yet, let your computer do it for you. Word processing programs will check your manuscript for readability. The scan identifies words of three syllables or longer, wordy sentences and lengthy paragraphs—elements that diminish understanding.

These scales report the difficulty of your prose. As a rule, commercial writing should never surpass a reading level of twelfth grade. To me, a tenth-grade level pushes the envelope. Many writing coaches recommend a level of seventh to eighth grade. This book weighs in at 7.0 on one scale and 8.2 on another, with an average of 14 words in each sentence and two sentences for each paragraph. Fewer than 5 percent of sentences use passive voice—and some of those are examples.

The notion of reading difficulty can lead to flaming disputes between writers and writing teachers because readability tends to be arbitrary. I won't join the debate between art and artifice except to say that, as a beginning writer, you'd be taking a big risk if you wrote in a dense, complex style suitable for college graduates only.

## STEP 31: READ YOUR MATERIAL ALOUD

Into a tape recorder. As you play back your scenes, listen for the following:

✓ **Excessive musings.** When a character starts brainstorming with herself, weighing options and grappling with decisions, she's musing. By itself, this isn't objectionable in brief passages. When you see musing that's rambled on for half a page, you've crossed a line. Ask yourself whether such internal monologue might better be put into action, dialogue or the trash bin.

✓ **Droning explanations.** If you hear an explanation that sounds like a classroom lecture, recast the passage.

✓ **Tongue twisters.** Fix.

✓ **Repetitions.** Cut.

✓ **Faulty rhythm.** If the material sounds choppy when you read it, although there's no coinciding action, smooth out the passage. If it drones on, you'll hear it.

✓ **Narcoleptic passages.** If the passage's content bores even you, start rewriting. Juice it up or cut it out.

√ **Narrative blunders.** If you commit sins against the fictional truth you've established, you'll hear them on tape.

√ **Strained emphasis.** If you hear yourself putting on too much of a radio voice to make a passage understood, you'll know the words on the page can't carry the freight alone. You have some rewriting to do.

When you're finished editing this draft of your first master scene, your writing ought to sing.

## STEP 32: WRITE YOUR REMAINING MASTER SCENES

Same deal. This time, though, I doubt you'll make even a fraction of the amateur errors you did on the first scene.

In any case, write, revise and move on to one master scene after another. When you've finished, you'll have a completed main story line. I assure you, you'll be enough of a polished writer by this time to breeze through the remaining steps.

## STEP 33: TIE THE REST OF THE NOVEL
## INTO THE MAIN STORY LINE

Subplots, minor scenes and narrative connections will fall into line as you proceed because the primary work is done. You'll have developed a sense for how much detail you'll need to enrich the story without letting it drag or detour excessively. You'll have a stack of fix cards to guide you in tying up loose ends.

Submit each new scene and narrative passage to the same revision standards as your master scenes.

Run an occasional word count on the manuscript. If you stay tuned to your novel's length, you'll be sure to avoid overwriting—remember 70,000 to 80,000 is about right for most fiction categories. If it looks like you'll be short on word count, pump up the conflict in important scenes rather than padding out narration. If you're long, at least you know you've finished the main story line. You can keep the rest of the novel lean without damaging the story.

## STEP 34: READ THE COMPLETED MANUSCRIPT ALOUD

Again. This time reading from a paper printout. I can't explain why, but reading your novel in hard copy creates a different impression than reading it on screen does. Even for you, the writer. This activity will reveal aspects of your manuscript you can't see, except on paper.

Either dictate the story into a tape recorder or read with a trusted friend to share the reading and to add vital criticism. Make your corrections on screen.

## STEP 35: EDIT USING THE GAP METHOD

A seemingly mechanical process that yields priceless artistic results. The final draft of a novel has yet to be written that can't be improved using the GAP method.

GAP stands for "gain a page." You try to shorten every chapter by one page. You do this by gaining a line in every paragraph in your novel. That's all there is to it.

### The GAP method

**Work on screen.** GAP doesn't work as well on paper because you can't see the result immediately.

**Work on an electronic copy** of your manuscript. Save your original file, backing it up on disk or cartridge. Identify the working file as a GAP version. Since this edit is a cutting exercise, you'll chop words and phrases at first. As you become bolder, you'll excise sentences and paragraphs. Before long, you'll be slashing whole scenes. If you change your mind and want to restore material, refer to the original file. Although it seems as if you're only reducing word count, you will find a substantial increase in clarity as well.

**Note the number of pages** in your chapters as you go.

**Run the first GAP edit.** Shorten every paragraph by at least one line. Sometimes, when the last line of a paragraph is only one word, you can delete a single word anywhere in the paragraph. Your word processing software moves the remaining words up to fill in the gap, and you gain a line. If the final line in a paragraph extends from margin to margin, you have to work at it. You cut a word here, a syllable there—nothing. You replace a long word with a shorter word—no luck. You recast the sentence—still no line gained. You discover that you can't shorten a three-line paragraph to two lines.

No problem. Just performing the exercise has improved that paragraph. Guaranteed. Note: If you make changes that must be applied elsewhere in the manuscript, remember to write reminders to yourself on fix cards and apply those changes throughout.

Most of all, don't get hung up on the feeling that this seems like a purely mechanical drill. Fact is, even if you're already within the prescribed word count, this exercise will improve the quality of your editing. Why? Because it forces you to focus on a goal that's visual, measurable and capable of delivering instant gratification—you can see the results.

Once you set your mind to thoughtfully cutting words, lines, paragraphs and pages, the best of your writing will emerge from any fog on the page. Rather than thinking "This paragraph doesn't sound so bad; I'll leave it in and see what an editor thinks," you'll be saying to yourself, "If I cut this phrase and find one strong word to replace a string of four weaker words, I can gain a line, maybe even a page."

Although you're concentrating on method, your art will blossom. Your sentences will snap. Your paragraphs will sing. Your scenes will come alive. Prove it to yourself. Try this exercise on a single master scene. Ask a trusted colleague to read both the original and the GAP-edited version and render an opinion about which is better. I already know the answer.

When you're finished, count the number of pages saved. Congratulate yourself, especially if you shortened each chapter by more than 5 percent. But you're not finished.

**Run a second GAP edit.** Try doubling the number of pages you gained on the first run. It can be done.

Then put the novel aside. Come back to it in a week or two, when your blood is running cold again.

**Run a third GAP edit.** This time, try for the same number of pages you gained on GAP one—you don't want to find yourself cutting past the fat and into the muscle. Don't rush. Make your final-final cuts deliberate and thoughtful.

**Run a word count.** If you've still not achieved a word count that's longer than novels in the category you're writing, sorry. You'll just have to keep cutting. Even Stephen King, whose rerelease of *The Stand* set a new standard for novels the size and weight of cinder blocks, couldn't pull that off with his first published tale, *Carrie*. What chance do you have?

On later books, your contract will specify minimum and maximum count. The contract for this book mandated 38,000 to 42,000. My first draft exceeded 50,000 words, requiring me to GAP cut by a minimum of 8,000 words. I sliced deeper so I could achieve a leaner book, submitting 41,000 words. This allowed my editor freedom either to cut or to ask me to deal with topics I hadn't originally included in the book. Overwriting by 20 percent doesn't seem outrageous to me.

Underwriting is another issue altogether. When I was writing feature material for newspapers, nothing was tougher than padding a story to meet a minimum word count. I hope that doesn't happen to you. If it does, I think it would be better to submit a compact story than to fluff out the manuscript.

Either way, when your novel reaches an acceptable final word count, it's time to sell it to an editor or agent.

# 6 PREPARE YOUR NOVEL FOR SALE

### 5 tips for breaking into the marketplace

> Nothing stinks like a pile of unpublished writing.
>
> Sylvia Plath

It ain't art anymore—it's bidness. Forget everything you ever learned in your literature classes about musical language, symbolism and theme. Put aside any ideas I may have planted about characterization, pace and rhythm. From now on, it's selling—naked commerce—not much different from peddling fruit and vegetables from your garden: The produce has to be good, and it must be presented well. If your peaches look wonderful but taste bland and woody, it's no sale. If the tomatoes are blemished and stinky besides, nobody cares that they were organically grown in soil imported from the Nile Delta.

> **Cardinal Rule #37:** Sell your novel not with the idea that publishers should give you and your agent money for it, but with the notion that buying your manuscript will make money for them.

You won't find many guarantees in publishing, but here's one you can take to the bank: If an agent believes she can make money selling your novel to a publisher, she'll handle it; if a publisher believes she can make money selling your novel to the public, she'll buy it. Period.

Now, how to get their minds right.

Once you get it into your skull that you must sell your product to every level of the industry, you've taken a huge first step.

Start by understanding the people you must sell to within a literary agency or a publishing house. People at every level can reject you. Here's a typical journey for material you submit.

**Mail handler.** This person opens and sorts mail and directs it to the proper recipient. Even she might have rejection authority. If the agency or house has a rule of accepting query letters only, she'll send back an unsolicited, completed manuscript. You wasted all that postage and nobody ever read a word of your novel.

**First reader.** This is usually an entry-level employee, intern or outside person hired to screen out the chaff. Fully 80 to 90 percent of material will be rejected at this level.

**Associate.** An assistant or secretary will sometimes screen material for an editor or agent. The associate will likely have veto power on anything sent up by a first reader—which means the associate can reject. He might also add remarks, highlight intriguing queries and forward your material. He might also have authority to request that sample chapters or a full manuscript be sent to his attention.

**Editor or agent.** She'll skim your material and either reject it or ask for more. Will she buy your material if she likes it? Not right away. The selling job goes on. She will probably ask another editor or agent in house to read the material. If both agree on the material's potential, they'll present a package to a company acquisitions meeting. Whether in a publishing house or an agency, your manuscript will be evaluated for its sales potential, marketing strategy, budget, cover art and other business considerations, including the amount of money you might receive for your work.

You won't attend the acquisitions meeting, so why am I telling you about it? To remind you of the nature of this process: business, selling, money. No matter how well it is written, unless an agency or publishing house can muster a reasonable expectation of making money on your manuscript, it will likely be rejected. As they say in the Mafia movies: "Nuttin' personal; just business."

You may never discover why you get rejected at any stage of the proceedings. Some possibilities: lack of time, lack of focus, lack of talent, lack of SASE, lack of a market. Others: The book's not right for the house or agency, or the list of books or authors in a category is full. Sometimes there's no reason, just bad luck.

How can you overcome such a wall of obstacles? Two things: good writing and adherence to the next cardinal rule.

> **Cardinal Rule #38:** Don't waste people's time.

Nothing but cash flow is more valuable than time in the publishing business—a high-energy industry filled with deadlines and juggling of projects. Every contact you make should indicate you're not going to waste anybody's time. That's the philosophy behind the five steps that follow.

## STEP 1: IDENTIFY A DOZEN DEALERS FOR YOUR PRODUCT

Pick six at first. Either six agents or six publishing houses. Check the current directories. Read every entry. Identify all the people who either publish or represent material like you've written. Narrow your list. Recheck the directory entries so you know exactly what each agency or house demands in the way of contacts, SASE and the like.

Should you market to agents or send your materials to publishers? Not to be wishy-washy, but I feel strongly both ways. If you get an offer of a contract from a publisher, you'll be able to obtain an agent over the phone. If you find an agent to represent you, the job of selling now belongs to him and you can continue writing.

My advice? Market to six agents. After the last of those sales letters has gone out, market to six publishing houses.

## STEP 2: IDENTIFY THREE DISTINCTIVE ASPECTS OF YOUR NOVEL

As always, think business. How is your novel different from what's already in the marketplace, yet not too different?

> **Cardinal Rule #39:** Sell your novel as fresh, distinctive and radically new—but not radical.

As a rule, publishing, being a business, isn't overpopulated with mavericks and gamblers. Whereas lots of editors have lost their jobs for buying stinkers, nobody ever got fired for rejecting a manuscript from an unknown. Strip away the glamorous aura they generate about themselves and giant publishing houses will look like your garden-variety plastic manufacturer—with executive trolls trying to climb their career fire poles and the grunts just trying to eke out a living. Try to persuade, not overpower, always adhering to the logic that fresh material will improve the publisher's lot in life.

Identify your novel's distinguishing elements. If it's a western, maybe you took an original approach of realism rather than romanticizing the Old West. If you were able to add authenticity because you spent last fall rounding up cattle in Montana, by all means highlight that.

Suppose you wrote a romance about high school sweethearts whose twenty-year marriage had to end in divorce before they could fall in love at the adult level? That might be a fresh twist.

If you're an expert in a field that's been woven into your novel's fabric, you'll want to identify that as a distinctive aspect.

Is your novel based on a historical event? A new science? A new take on an old science? An unsolved crime? That's distinctive.

If you know of a growing market trend or regional news event that hasn't gone national, tell somebody.

If any aspect of your novel is likely to make money for the publisher or agent, by all means, identify it in your first contact.

## STEP 3: WRITE A TARGETED KILLER
## SALES LETTER—ONE PAGE MAX

Two considerations apply to targeting. First, address your sales letter to a specific person. Phone the agency or publishing house and ask whether the agent or editor listed in the directory still works there. If so, ask if she has a new job title. If not, ask for a name of somebody new who's accepting submissions. The idea is to avoid mailing in the blind to "Whom it May Concern," "The Editor" or "Mr. Agent Man."

Second, review each directory entry to be sure you're sending precisely the package the company wishes to see. If the agency wants a one-page cover letter and the first twenty-five pages, send that (and not twenty-five pages from the middle of the book, either). If it's letter and synopsis only, don't send a writing sample—the first impression you create will be either that you *can't* follow instructions or that you *won't*. Neither is good.

## The three-part sales letter

**Part One—Open with your nugget statement.** You already wrote your first paragraph in chapter one. Rewrite it in letter form:

> Please consider (publishing/representing) my romance novel, *Heart of Lead*. My story is about (write in your nugget statement).

This tells the agent or editor what you're selling without wasting time on introductions. If you've written a snappy nugget, it will act as a sample of your ability. Now is not the time to stretch your summary to one hundred words.

**Part Two—Tell why your novel is distinctive** enough to make money for the agency or publishing house. Be artful about it. Don't say something like "My novel is going to make us all rich." Rather, point out what's new, what's fresh, what's different. Tell who will read the novel, an audience that the publisher might not have considered. If you've thought of a business consideration that's not apparent in a reading of the nugget, bring it up.

**Part Three—Give the pertinent details.** Essentials include a mention that the novel is completed, the word length and pertinent biographical information. That means if you've published articles or books, say so. If you're an expert in a pertinent field, tell somebody.

Don't ramble. Keep this letter to one page. If the material is enticing, and your writing is coherent, the letter will do its job of selling. Extending your sales pitch to ten pages won't help.

Your last words should—in the words of sales trainers—ask for the sale. Appeal for a decision by the editor or agent: "May I send you a writing sample?" Or the first three chapters. Or the completed manuscript. Something that requires a response.

## STEP 4: ENCLOSE A KILLER SYNOPSIS—AGAIN, ONE PAGE

Flesh out your nugget statement to one page, double-spaced. Introduce your adversaries and keep to the main plot line—you don't want to muddle your sales pitch with endless subplots. Tell about the most exciting scenes in the novel. Reveal the ending. Don't be coy, as in: "Want to see how it turns out?" All that does is antagonize.

Finally, enclose an SASE (self-addressed, stamped envelope) so the agent or editor can either send a note asking for more material or break your heart with a rejection slip. Use a business-size envelope.

But don't enclose postage for returning writing samples. Instead, send out freshly printed material every time. Saving the return postage will pay for printing, and you won't have to worry about dog-eared pages creating a negative impression on a second submission.

## STEP 5: GET ON WITH YOUR LIFE
Waiting for a response is the worst aspect of this business. I've had editors take thirteen months to respond to a sales letter. Here are worthwhile activities for passing time.

**Start a log for your submissions.** Keep track of dates sent, items you sent in a given package, rejections, names of editors and agents, houses, postage and so on. Figure eleven is a sample to copy and keep in your Writer's Tool Kit.

| Submission History of | | | | | | | | | | | |
|---|---|---|---|---|---|---|---|---|---|---|---|
| Date Out | Name | House/Agency | Ltr | Cost | Smpl | Synps | Prpsl | Ms | Response | Date Done | Done |
| | | | | | | | | | | | ☐ |
| | | | | | | | | | | | |

*Fig. 11. Submission log*

**Get busy on another novel.** Nothing occupies the mind more productively. Should you sell the first, you'll be able to offer the second book in progress. If you sell the second, you'll be able to remarket the first, unsold novel.

> **Cardinal Rule #40:** To improve your writing, write.

Everybody knows that professionals can't afford to let their talents atrophy: Pianists keep sharp with constant practice, dancers dance, ballplayers hit, golfers swing and singers sing. Yet the last thing the would-be writer wants to do is write.

Every professional writer worthy of name knows you can't make a dime in the business without planting your butt in a chair and writing. So do.

**Should you receive nothing but rejections,** review your sales letter, especially the aspects of your novel you thought were so distinctive. Try to find other, more mercenary, aspects to tout in your next round of letters. Send a second dozen sales letters, half to agents, half to editors.

Should a rejection be personalized, try to glean something of value from it. Heck, just because they're rejections doesn't mean they're bad. I once received a rejection that included these words:

> . . . compelling . . . well written . . . really jumps with energy . . . I encourage you to send it to places like Avon, Bantam or Dell.

I photocopied the rejection and sent it with a sales letter to all three publishers. Dell bought the novel, my first. Later I used it to sell *Writer's Digest* a story titled "Turning Rejections Into Royalties," published in the October 1988 issue. I'm using it again as a closing anecdote in this book—a lot of mileage for one rejection letter.

**Should you be asked to send more material,** follow instructions to the letter. Double-check your package before you mail it. On the outside of the envelope, write in bold letters "Requested Material." That will prevent those pesky mail handlers and first readers from rejecting you out of hand. For the same reason, the first line of your cover letter on second contact should read "Here's the material you asked to see." Won't that be a thrill to write?

Now get busy. And good luck.

# APPENDIX

## THE CARDINAL RULES

1. Never be boring, not for one scene, paragraph, sentence or word.
2. Every writing rule in the book has an exception—except for Cardinal Rule #1.
3. Begin with the end in mind.
4. If you don't envision a truly heroic character with heroic goals, on an action-packed journey, encountering obstacles and a worthy opponent and arriving alive and wiser at the end of your novel after having engaged in a titanic struggle, it's not likely your novel will be seriously considered in the publishing business.
5. Finish your novel before you make the first attempt to sell it.
6. At the minimum, you should have three master characters for your novel. At the maximum, you should have three.
7. Your novel plays out in relation to the world of your heroic character. If an action, setting or other character does not relate to the heroic character—either as a cause or an effect—odds are, that action, setting or character doesn't belong in the novel.
8. Think of your novel as a heroic character's universe clashing with his adversary's universe and you will have distilled the business of writing a novel to its essence.
9. Never get sidetracked on issues such as exhaustive biographical sketches and detailed physical settings. Do all your important writing in your novel, not in preparation.
10. A heroic character's goals and motivations cannot lead to trivial pursuits. Master characters must be given to furious passions, driving forces, lifetime ambitions and fundamental values. A character must be willing to risk all, even life, for such things.
11. The central conflict in a novel arises from the powerful, usually violent struggle between the opposing goals and motivations of the heroic character and his adversary.
12. Even the most heroic character is somehow flawed, often seriously, and the nastiest villain has some saving grace, no matter how small.
13. Give major characters—and even minor characters—goals and motivations of their own. Permit them to have personal reasons for being

in your novel rather than using them as set pieces for your convenience.

14. Begin your novel by writing the climactic scene first.

15. No scene in your novel is as important as your climax. Every scene that precedes the climax must logically build toward it, and every scene that follows the climax to the end of the story must be a logical result of it.

16. When contemplating a scene, if you can't clearly establish the purpose for a scene, *don't create that scene.* Use narration to make your point and convey your readership to the next scene.

17. What matters is not so much what people say when they pick up your novel as what they say after they put it down.

18. Anytime in the course of a novel that the story changes direction because of problems introduced or complications resolved between master characters, write it as a master scene.

19. You elevate the grand-scale pace of your novel by bunching master scenes; likewise, you relax that pace by inserting major scenes, minor scenes and various narrative devices between your master scenes.

20. A subplot *must* establish a direct connection to the main story line, advancing and complicating the story. If a subplot is a parallel issue that never affects the outcome of the main story line in a *significant* way, leave it out.

21. Write your favorite master scene first. After you've revised that scene, choose your next favorite master scene. And so on, until you've written an entire first draft of your novel as master scenes.

22. No matter what form of concordance you employ, always use fix cards. Fix cards will clear your mind of mechanical trivialities, leaving it free to concentrate on the act of creation.

23. Use a third-person, past-tense point of view (POV), and limit the novel's omniscience to your master characters.

24. Study best-selling writing by copying selected segments of your favorite best-selling author's novel word for word.

25. Always try using verbs and nouns before resorting to adjectives and adverbs. A concrete noun partnered with a precise verb will kick butt on adjectives and adverbs any day of the week.

26. Write to suit yourself.

27. Build action into every scene, every passage of dialogue, every sentence of your novel. When in doubt, use action.

28. Capitalize on conflict. Assert it in every scene of your novel, never allowing it to fall below a discernible level of tension.

29. If a line of dialogue doesn't indicate conflict or isn't leading up to conflict, don't bother writing it. Use some other narrative device.

30. Rather than describe, create powerful images.

31. Research only as much as necessary to enrich your novel with reality or, even better, a sense of wonder or discovery. Never include data for its own sake or, worse, to show how brilliant you are.

32. Take a stand. Avoid splitting hairs in images and emotions, especially in master scenes. Dramatize. Exaggerate. Embellish facts. Clarify your fictional truths.

33. Once you clarify images and emotions, be consistent with the stand you've taken. Never change on whimsy or by coincidence. Once established, only the characters influenced by their realistic, competing motivations—and not the author—can reorder images and emotions.

34. Play fair. Don't withhold details crucial to understanding the story just so you can spring a surprise later.

35. Maintain singularity: one idea for each sentence; a single topic for each paragraph; a singular plot point for each scene. And stick to the main story line in writing your novel's first draft.

36. Achieve dramatic effect by adding snap—power words, quick pace and high emotion—to the ends of your critical sentences, paragraphs and scenes.

37. Sell your novel not with the idea that publishers should give you and your agent money for it, but with the notion that buying your manuscript will make money for them.

38. Don't waste people's time.

39. Sell your novel as fresh, distinctive and radically new—but not radical.

40. To improve your writing, write.

## INDEX